STEELPAN IN EDUCATION

STEELPAN IN EDUCATION

A HISTORY OF THE NORTHERN ILLINOIS UNIVERSITY STEELBAND

ANDREW MARTIN   RAY FUNK   JEANNINE REMY

NIU Press / DeKalb IL

Northern Illinois University Press, DeKalb 60115
© 2017 by Northern Illinois University Press
All rights reserved

26 25 24 23 22 21 20 19 18 17   1 2 3 4 5
978-0-87580-778-2 (paper)
978-1-60909-237-5 (e-book)
Book and cover design by Yuni Dorr

Library of Congress Cataloging-in-Publication Data
Names: Martin, Andrew R., author. | Funk, Ray, author. | Remy, Jeannine, author.
Title: Steelpan in education : a history of the Northern Illinois University Steelband / Andrew Martin, Ray Funk, and Jeannine Remy.
Description: DeKalb : Northern Illinois University Press, [2017] | Includes bibliographical references and index.
Identifiers: LCCN 2017034857 (print) | LCCN 2017035116 (ebook) | ISBN 9781609092375 (ebook) | ISBN 9780875807782 (pbk. : alk. paper)
Subjects: LCSH: Northern Illinois University. Steelband—History. | Steel bands (Music)—Illinois—De Kalb—History.
Classification: LCC ML28.D4 (ebook) | LCC ML28.D4 N674 2017 (print) | DDC 785/.68—dc23
LC record available at https://lccn.loc.gov/2017034857

CONTENTS

Illustrations vii
Foreword ix
Acknowledgments xi

      CHAPTER 1   INTRODUCTION 3

      CHAPTER 2   AL O'CONNOR'S LIFE BEFORE STEELPAN 11

      CHAPTER 3   FROM HUMMINGBIRD TO HUSKY 21

      CHAPTER 4   THE O'CONNOR/ALEXIS ERA AND THE NIU/BIRCH CREEK CONNECTION 33

      CHAPTER 5   GUEST ARTISTS THROUGHOUT THE YEARS 47

      CHAPTER 6   ON THE ROAD—THE NIU STEELBAND TOURS AMERICA 55

      CHAPTER 7   PANNING TO THE EAST—THE NIU STEELBAND CAPTURES ASIA 65

      CHAPTER 8   THE PAGANINI OF PAN, LIAM TEAGUE, COMES TO NIU 79

      CHAPTER 9   RETURN TO TRINIDAD AND THE WORLD STEELBAND MUSIC FESTIVAL 2000 89

      CHAPTER 10   STEELPAN DEGREE PROGRAM AND THE NIU/UWI PIPELINE 97

      CHAPTER 11   O'CONNOR RETIRES, TEAGUE/ALEXIS ERA BEGINS 103

      CHAPTER 12   EPILOGUE—THE NIU STEELBAND INTO THE FUTURE 117

Appendix One 125
Appendix Two 131
Notes 137
Index 149

ILLUSTRATIONS

FIGURE 1.1	NIU Steelband Concert Rehearsal (2012) 4
FIGURE 2.1	Al O'Connor Playing New steelpans (1970s) 15
FIGURE 2.2	First NIU Steelband Concert Press Release (1974) 16
FIGURE 2.3	Setting up for Performance (circa 1976) 18
FIGURE 3.1	Trinidad and Tobago National Steel Orchestra (1964) 25
FIGURE 3.2	Cliff Alexis working at St. Paul Central High School (1970s) 28
FIGURE 3.3	NIU Steelband playing Cliff Alexis made steelpans (circa early 1980s) 30
FIGURE 4.1	"Little Band" Steelband Promotional Card (early 1980s) 35
FIGURE 4.2	Birch Creek Steelband (mid 1980s) 39
FIGURE 5.1	NIU Steelband with Andy Narell (1985) 50
FIGURE 5.2	NIU Steelband with Leonard Moses 51
FIGURE 6.1	NIU Steelband Album Cover Photo (1976) 58
FIGURE 7.1	NIU Steelband CSK Hall Performance, Taiwan (1992) 69
FIGURE 7.2	NIU Steelband performing at Seoul Drum Festival, Korea (2002) 77
FIGURE 8.1	Liam Teague and Lester Trilla at the Trilla Steel Drum Factory (late 1990s) 86
FIGURE 9.1	World Steelband Music Festival Competition performance (2000) 93
FIGURE 10.1	Liam Teague as Graduate Student Concertizing in Taiwan (late 1990s) 101
FIGURE 12.1	Cliff Alexis, Les Trilla, Al O'Connor (1999) 118
FIGURE 12.2	NIU Steelband at Virginia Beach, PANFest (2016) 120

FOREWORD

"Why are you messing around with this? It's never going to go anywhere."

This is what was said to me by two of my colleagues after the NIU Steelband became the first steelband to ever perform at a Percussive Arts Society International Convention. This one was held at the University of Tennessee/Knoxville during the fall of 1977. Their reaction was not typical of most of the audience that attended, but I continued to find it amusing to recall as our program continued to grow and progress.

I came to Northern Illinois University in the fall of 1968 as Instructor of Percussion, always with the idea of starting a steelband after seeing several perform in the US Virgin Islands and seeing the effect that these magical instruments had on both the players and the audience. Everyone was incapable of standing still; sometimes the panmen were far more agitated than those listening.

I had always felt that having a group like this as part of a percussion program would be a tremendous value to the students, as they would be able to experience how making music can be a joy for anyone. The bands I was fortunate to play with might have a secretary from the prime minister's office standing on one side of me and a dock worker on the other side. All were conscious of the same thing—making music so precise and energetic as to almost create an out-of-body experience.

Our program took some giant steps forward with the additions of Clifford Alexis in 1985, and Liam Teague in 1992 (originally as a student) and the introduction of the bachelor's and master's degrees with the steelpan as the major instrument. We began to attract students from the Caribbean (mostly from Trinidad and Tobago), Canada, Japan, Denmark, and Brazil as well as from all over the United States. This was due in large part to the scholarship support of Lester Trilla and the Trilla Steel Drum Corporation, whose backing of the program continues to this day. It also attracted the attention of steelpan junkies Andrew Martin, Ray Funk, and Jeannine Remy, all known authorities in this art form. In this excellent publication they have admirably assembled a history and documentary of the NIU Steelband and those responsible for its formation and continuous evolution.

As you read this book, I would strongly urge you to remember that this band, when formed, was considered the first actively performing steelband in an American university. What it has become today is extraordinary. And remember, "It's never going to go anywhere!"

G. Allan O'Connor
Director Emeritus, NIU Steelband
2014 recipient of the Percussive Arts Society
Lifetime Achievement Award

ACKNOWLEDGMENTS

The following pages were made possible through the personal contributions of many individuals, spread out over three continents, too numerous to list. We would like to recognize the efforts of NIU Steelband alumni and supporters Michael Bento, Shannon Dudley, Scott McConnell, Kuo-Huang Han, Satanand Sharma, Paul Ross, James Walker, Elizabeth DeLamater, Mike Schwebke, Mia Gormandy, Adam Grise, Harold Headley, Lester Trilla, Kenneth Joseph, Seion Gomez, Jan Bach, Charissa Granger, and Leonard Moses for their work, perspectives, and consultation. The graciousness and patience demonstrated by those men and women throughout this process are a testament to their continued dedication and love of the artistry of steelpan and the NIU steelband program. Furthermore, we are particularly thankful for the contributions of Sarah Barnes-Tsai and Yuko Asada for their help in tracking down documents and photos and for their insights.

A project such as this could never flourish without the support of Northern Illinois University, and to this end the support of Rich Holly, Robert Chappell, Barry Mannette, and Khan Cordice was invaluable to our book's completion and success. We would like to further acknowledge all the players, past and present, who contributed through the decades toward the international growth and development of the NIU Steelband through their tenure with the band and their dedication to the program. Because of their talent and dedication, the reputation and prestige of the NIU Steelband holds historical and educational value at the tertiary level, and the band continues to be a flagship ensemble of international acclaim as ambassadors in ethnic music and cultural studies in academia.

In Trinidad, we would like to thank the University of the West Indies—St. Augustine, Pan Trinbago, and the American Embassy for their continued support of the NIU steelband program. We are also indebted to several colleagues, including Brandon Haskett, James Campbell, and Chris Tanner, for their helpful suggestions, comments, and editorial guidance throughout the research and writing of this book. Their expert knowledge of steelband history and the American steelband scene respectively made this a better book in all regards.

Finally, for more than forty years the NIU Steelband has been the vision and passion of three men who have greatly advanced the art form and culture of steelband. As such, the graciousness, openness, and unwavering support of G. Allan O'Connor, Clifford Alexis, and Liam Teague made this book possible, and we authors are honored to be able to share their story.

Andrew Martin, Ray Funk, Jeannine Remy

STEELPAN IN EDUCATION

CHAPTER 1
INTRODUCTION

> If anybody had told me when I started messing around with this [steelband] in 1973 that we'd be at the point we're at right now, I would basically tell them they were out of their minds.
>
> —Al O'Connor (2003)[1]

From the moment you step off the airplane, the experience of visiting Port of Spain, Trinidad and DeKalb, Illinois during the winter is a study in contrasts. For travelers from the north typically arriving in the evening to Piarco International Airport in Trinidad, the air-conditioned terminal fails to mask the impending shock of oven-like heat that blasts visitors exiting the airport doors to the taxi stand. After surviving the roughly forty-minute maxi-taxi ride from the airport to the city of Port of Spain, one arrives at steelpan mecca—panyards saturate the city and surrounding area, and the Queen's Park Savannah located in the northwest part of downtown is the epicenter. During January and February, Trinidad (and its sister island Tobago) is bustling with energy. The Carnival season is fast approaching, and countless residents are making preparations for the Panorama steelband competition, masquerade (mas') bands, calypso tents, competitions of all sorts, and the extensive weekend activities ranging from Kiddies Carnival, Panorama Finals, Dimanche Gras into Jouvert Monday and Carnival Tuesday. Considered the dry season by local standards, the temperature is hot and the humidity is oppressive. The daily temperature of equatorial Trinidad is relatively consistent, regardless of season, and visiting steelpan enthusiasts from the north, Europe, and Asia are not spared the blistering daytime sun. Midday finds local

Trinidadian vendors tending food stands in preparation for the evening when, spared the afternoon sun, flurries of activity commence as the people emerge to take advantage of more temperate evening temperatures.

The hundreds of steelbands that saturate the island are busy too. The Panorama preliminaries are underway, and the lucky bands still alive in the competition can be heard nightly rehearsing in outdoor panyards that dot the cities and countryside. Weeks later, during the Panorama semi-final competition held in the Queen's Park Savannah in Port of Spain, the catchy melodies of soca/calypso tunes, chosen by steelbands as their song-of-the-year arrangements for the massive steelbands, are everywhere. The tunes waft in and out from various steelbands and blare from the park's massive sound system and passing car stereos. For several months leading up to Carnival each year, steelbands capture the ears and hearts of Trinidad's approximately one million inhabitants and many more expatriates living in the extended diaspora of Toronto, London, and New York.

February in DeKalb, by contrast, greets visitors with a starkly different reality. Exiting O'Hare International Airport in suburban Chicago during winter introduces one to the bone-chilling winds blowing off Lake Michigan. From the icy and snow-drifted taxi stand, Interstate 294 gives way to Interstate 88 as visitors are initiated to the towering concrete ramparts and high speeds of Illinois freeways. Traveling west on Interstate 88, the concrete and hustle and bustle of Chicago suburbs melts away, and after roughly an hour of driving, the suburbs gradually give way to the rolling cornfields of rural Illinois, which appear to

FIGURE 1.1. NIU Steelband Concert Rehearsal (2012) (Continued on next page)

stretch for as long as the eye can see. The quiet serenity of the farms dotting the countryside is interrupted by the city of DeKalb, and as the visitor pulls off the interstate the only thing separating him from America's de facto steelband mecca is a few acres of plowed cornfields covered in snow. Upon arriving in DeKalb for the first time in January of 1993, Liam Teague recalled, "Al and Cliff picked me up from the airport; it was cold and we drove for what seemed like hours. Cliff was hungry, and we stopped at a McDonald's, and I remember hearing people in the McDonald's swearing and using foul language. I was shocked by this for some reason. I stared out the window of our booth and a snowstorm had hit. This was the first time I had ever seen snow. As I watched the blowing snow from that McDonald's, I recall thinking, "Dear God, what have I done? Why did I leave Trinidad?"[2]

Steelpan—What Is It?

This is the story of how a university music program in the heartland of America became one of the most important hotbeds for the development of a new Caribbean musical instrument called the steelpan. The steelpan is a tuned idiophone created out of recycled 55-gallon oil barrels; it was invented in Trinidad and Tobago sometime in the late 1930s and further developed in the decades that followed. An instrument with many names, outside of Trinidad and Tobago the steelpan is sometimes called the "steel drum," and in Trinidad

and Tobago the favored term for the instrument is the "steelpan" or "pan." Steelpans are grouped into sets and are conceived of in families called "steelbands," which feature a mix of variations spanning high-pitch single steelpans to low-pitched multi-drum sets of instruments. Culturally and musically, steelbands descend from West African drumming and bamboo-stomping ensembles called "Tamboo Bamboo," which historically provided parade music for Afro-Trinidadians during Carnival. Due in part to British colonial laws from the 1880s that banned the playing of drums and the like, Trinidadians transferred their Tamboo Bamboo rhythms to making music on paint cans, biscuit tins, and other types of metal containers before finally settling on oil drums sometime in the mid- to late 1930s. The United States has had a presence in Trinidad and Tobago since the Roosevelt administration's "Destroyers for Bases Agreement" program in 1940.[3] The US government traded old naval destroyer ships to Britain in exchange for swaths of land in various British colonies and territories (including Trinidad). The US military built the Chaguaramas military base on the northwestern tip of the island in 1942. Discarded oil drums, prime material for making steelpans, were abundant around the base and immediately became a favored source of material for steelpan construction.[4]

The Trinidadian steelband climate of the 1940s and early 1950s was driven in part by rivalry and turf warfare waged by the so-called "bad johns" found in Port of Spain's tight-knit neighborhoods, and techniques for building steelpans were closely guarded secrets. Unemployed lower-class Trinidadians spent years toiling in panyards, creating and refining the instrument, and it is this class of craftsman that is responsible for the lion's share of innovations in steelpan construction, building, and tuning.[5] Despite the efforts and dedication of poor and working-class peoples, steelpan and steelbands achieved an entirely new level of social and cultural importance in the early 1950s as the growing Trinidadian middle-class adopted the art form and became increasingly involved in all areas of the steelband movement.

The acceptance of steelbands as a social and musical movement benefited greatly from the work and efforts of dance impresario Beryl McBurnie and the Trinidad All-Steel Percussion Orchestra. Dancer Beryl McBurnie founded the Little Carib Theatre in Port of Spain, and it was McBurnie who first arranged for steelbands (the Invaders Steel Orchestra and the Merry Makers Steel Orchestra) to perform in the context of legitimate theater. These early steelband performances at the Little Carib Theatre were an important gateway for the steelband to reach the power brokers of Trinidad and Tobago's middle class, cultural elites, and politicians as it was here that the "common folk rubbed shoulders with the elite" and the steelband was in full bloom as a cultural expression and serious art form.[6]

The Trinidad All-Steel Percussion Orchestra (hereafter TASPO) was another key agent in the development of steelpans and steelbands in Trinidad and Tobago. TASPO was an all-star steelband comprised of the best pannists from steelbands across Trinidad and Tobago assembled for the purpose of performing for the Festival of Britain in 1951. TASPO was the first Trinidadian steelband to perform in Europe and contributed greatly to the musical development of steelbands in Trinidad and Tobago via its leader Barbadian Lieutenant Joseph Griffith who demanded that the TASPO members standardize many of the steelpan sets used by the various band members.[7] TASPO would have lasting musical implications for the future of the steelband movement and its members, a who's who of steelband pioneers, including Ellie Mannette, Anthony Williams, Andrew de la Bastide, and Winston "Spree" Simon to name a few.

As Trinidad and Tobago moved into the 1950s, there was a marked effort by the middle class to embrace local arts, and participation in steelbands by college boys (middle-class, educated young men) became a means for earning street credibility and hipness.[8] With the formation of these steelbands comprised of middle-class individuals, many of which still exist today, including Starlift, Silver Stars, and Dixieland, the entire steelband movement gained a degree of social credibility that would eventually lead to many of the early steelbands becoming viable cultural institutions.

Why Steelpan? Why Northern Illinois?

How did Northern Illinois University (NIU) become an international hotbed for steelband? DeKalb and Port of Spain are approximately 2700 miles and several large bodies of water apart, yet they share an affinity for the national instrument of Trinidad and Tobago. The present state of steelpan education in primary schools, secondary schools, and university steelpan programs in America forms a thriving and robust scene: the strongest and most active climate in the steelpan's sixty-five-year history in America. In the past two decades steelbands have become increasingly popular additions to school curricula and after-school programs throughout the United States. The open arms of American universities proved a receptive outlet for steelband activity, though initially on a very small scale, following the implosion of the calypso craze and waning public interest in exotica during the late 1950s.[9]

Despite an initial flurry of activity in several isolated locations, a number of barriers hampered large-scale adoption of steelbands into academia prior to 1973. These included, but were not limited to, the availability of instruments and qualified individuals to tune them, the overwhelming size of Trinidadian-style steelbands, and the lack of qualified instructors in the United States. The Republic of Trinidad and Tobago achieved independence from Britain in 1962; however, until changes in United States laws that assisted immigration went into effect in 1965, political relations and dialogue between the United States and the newly postcolonial Trinidad temporarily slowed, and in some cases prohibited, university study-abroad programs.[10] These restrictions were the third factor that served to create unfavorable conditions for the fledgling art form of steelpan as it attempted to gain traction in academia.

The story of the NIU steelband program is a tale of what has become the most successful steelpan program at an American university to date. Due to the talent and dedication of Al O'Connor, Cliff Alexis, Liam Teague, and a plethora of NIU students, staff, and administration, the NIU Steelband was able to succeed where other steelband programs failed, or at least failed to germinate. Their success is no doubt a reflection of the talented people of NIU; yet it also points to larger issues in the development of steelband programs in the

American university system. Unlike the steelband movement in Trinidad and Tobago, the development of steelband in America is less a unified movement in terms of socioeconomic class disparities—the residual effects of colonialism notwithstanding as its impact has little to do with the diaspora playing steelpan in the United States. To this end regional developments in steelband stem nearly entirely from pioneering individual pannists forging new traditions, aided by the larger movement in American academia for multiculturalism and multicultural performing ensembles. As of the mid-2000s, steelband was the third most common non-Western performing ensemble in American universities, with over 100 universities nationwide housing steelbands.[11] The number has since rapidly expanded in the past decade as colleges and universities across the United States embrace the multicultural and musical versatility of the steelband.[12]

Research by leading music education scholars suggests that university administrators and/or music department chairs see value in the steelband and, for one reason or another, covet steelbands enough to invest the capital funds required to purchase the instruments.[13] Folksinger extraordinaire and avid steelband enthusiast Pete Seeger considered steelband as an educational tool that could develop both a strong sense of rhythm and an even stronger sense of community and cultural appreciation among steelband participants.[14] Regardless of the motivation, be it multiculturalism, cultural diversity, music education, community building, or what have you, the history of the NIU steelband program and its unique role within the overall educational mission of the university is a primary concern of this book.

In the June 27, 1999 edition of the *Chicago Tribune*, noted arts critic Howard Reich was charged with reviewing a recent concerto performance by steelpan virtuoso Liam Teague (who was, at the time, a recent NIU graduate) and the Chicago Sinfonietta. The performance was one of the first steelpan concerto performances with a notable American orchestra. Reich's prose encapsulates the unlikely reality of NIU's position as a steelpan mecca with the headline "Steel Pan Alley: To become a virtuoso on the steel drum, Liam Teague had to leave his native Trinidad to study in—where else?—DeKalb." Reich's review locates one of the central ironies of steelband education in the United States, in which regional sites such as DeKalb, Illinois are hotbeds of pedagogical activity whereas Trinidad and Tobago is, relatively speaking, lagging behind. Moreover, since Liam Teague, one of Trinidad and Tobago's most prominent and virtuosic steelpan heroes, is in part a product of American steelband training, the notion held by many Trinidadians that steelpan belongs to any one place, people, or culture is under fire.

The following pages tell the story of precisely how the NIU steelband program was built from nothing, only to rise up and achieve a storied tradition and legendary reputation unique among university percussion programs. The story begins with an examination of NIU steelband founder Al O'Connor and how he came to steelpan. Chapter 2 explores the genesis of the NIU steelband as well as O'Connor's early career path prior to discovering the steelpan. The first years of the NIU steelband were marked with many successes; however, by 1980 O'Connor was facing the heavy reality that maintaining a steelband in top shape was no small task. He was keenly aware that a steelband was like a piano and, in order to keep the instruments sounding their best, an in-house tuner would be necessary. A chance encounter with the US Navy Steel Band led O'Connor to Trinidadian Cliff Alexis who, at the time, was living and building steelpans in St. Paul, Minnesota. After a five-year period of negotiation, Alexis joined O'Connor as a faculty/staff member resident steelpan tuner/builder at NIU in 1985. Chapter 3 chronicles Alexis's journey from Trinidad to DeKalb and O'Connor's role in the process.

The NIU steelband program in its current form is a construct of the collective efforts of O'Connor and Alexis and their roles as defined over the course of years. Chapter 4 takes a look at the transformation of the NIU steelband program following Cliff Alexis's arrival with a specific focus on how the pair worked as a team. One offshoot of the early success of the NIU steelband was the Birch Creek summer steelband music camp in Egg Harbor in Door County, Wisconsin, founded by O'Connor in 1982. Chapter 4 further details the emerging roles and changing facets of the NIU steelband program both in DeKalb and off campus.

Since the inception of the percussion program at NIU in 1968, O'Connor (and later Alexis and Teague) felt very strongly that bringing guest artists to campus was an integral part of the NIU experience. The roster of guest artists brought in to work specifically with the NIU steelband reflects the development of the band over the course of its history. Chapter 5 discusses the various guest artists of the NIU steelband program and highlights some of the particularly important and eventful encounters.

In addition to the early East Coast tours of the 1970s, the NIU steelband embarked on several major trips outside the Chicagoland area over the course of its history. Aside from two tours of Taiwan (1992 and 1998) and the World Steelband Music Festival in Trinidad (2000), the NIU Steelband also trekked forth on notable tours to the PASIC (Percussive Arts Society International Convention) in 1981 (Indianapolis), 1987 (St. Louis), and 1994 (Atlanta), and the 1995 ASA (Acoustical Society of America) national meeting in St. Louis. Beyond the publicity and prestige generated by the NIU Steelband on these various tours, O'Connor and Alexis sought a hands-on educational experience for NIU steelband members; these tours served as a laboratory for experiencing life on the road as a professional musician. Chapter 6 offers a synopsis and highlights of the various tours.

Domestically, things were going well for the NIU steelband program, and O'Connor and Alexis spent the better part of the 1980s slowly earning the respect of the Trinidadian public and the steelpan community. But it was two highly successful tours to Taiwan in March of 1992 and again in 1998, along with a tour to Seoul, South Korea to perform at the 2002 World Cup and the fourth annual Seoul Drum Festival that solidified the NIU Steelband's international reputation. The 1992 tour was the first such tour for an American steelband, not to mention the first for the NIU Steelband. Chapter 7 revisits the band's time in Asia in order to examine its history and contextualize its impact on the future development and reputation of the NIU Steelband at home and abroad.

In November of 1989, O'Connor embarked on his first visit to Trinidad and Tobago. He was eager to take in the sights, sounds, and smells of the place to whose musical culture he was so devoted. Alexis had been singing the praises of his NIU colleague to the panmen of Trinidad and Tobago for some time and was eager to take O'Connor to the panyards and introduce him to the legends and pioneers of the craft. Little did O'Connor and Alexis know, however, that their trip to Trinidad and Tobago in 1989 would have such important and lasting ramifications for the steelband program at NIU: this was the trip in which O'Connor and Alexis first met steelpan virtuoso and future NIU steelband faculty member Liam Teague. Chapter 8 offers a history of Liam Teague's discovery and journey from ten-year-old Trinidadian steelpan prodigy to graduate student in steelpan performance at NIU.

From the time Alexis joined O'Connor at NIU in 1985, the pair someday hoped to bring the NIU Steelband to Trinidad and Tobago in order to show off the progress of steelpan music in the United States and to expose NIU students to the real flesh and blood of steelpan's roots. In October of 2000, the NIU Steelband finally got its chance to sojourn to the birthplace of steelpan as a participant in the World Steelband Music Festival (WSMF) competition. Chapter 9 chronicles the NIU Steelband's journey to Trinidad in October of 2000 and celebrates the band's triumphant second-place finish in the World Steelband Music Festival competition.

One of the most important factors spurring Alexis to join O'Connor in DeKalb in 1985 was the hope that someday NIU might establish a freestanding degree program in steelpan. O'Connor shared this vision, and the pair worked steadily over the course of several years to divorce steelpan from the overarching umbrella of percussion and to create a curriculum that put the steelpan on an equal footing with the violin, piano, or voice in the NIU School of Music. In 1991 Harold Headley was the first person to graduate NIU with a degree in percussion with an emphasis on steelpan. In 1993 the University of the West Indies–St. Augustine began offering degree programs in steelpan, and the institution quickly became a feeder school for NIU; the latter welcomed several University of the West Indies–St. Augustine undergraduates into its graduate-degree program. Chapter 10 analyzes the establishment of the steelpan degree at NIU as well as the NIU/University of the West Indies–St. Augustine connection and the mutual benefit to each institution.

From its humble beginnings in 1973 through the high-profile tours of the 1990s and 2000s, Al O'Connor and Cliff Alexis (and later Liam Teague) became for many the faces of steelband in academia in the United States. The NIU steelband program underwent major changes when, after thirty-five years of teaching and service to NIU, O'Connor decided to retire in the summer of 2003. Chapter 11 focuses on Liam Teague's transition from NIU music student to NIU faculty member as well as on the changing sound and mission of the NIU steelband program as the Teague/Alexis era began in 2003.

Chapter 12 brings the story of the program to the current day as Liam Teague has continued to be a major performing artist sought all over the world and the NIU steelband program has expanded and attracts and trains amazing players. This new generation of pannists is pushing the boundaries of the steelpan and plays ever-widening styles of music, ranging from classical to jazz to contemporary. Into the future, the pannists of NIU are tackling ever more challenging music on steelpan and are taking the instrument to places where it has never gone before.

CHAPTER 2

AL O'CONNOR'S LIFE BEFORE STEELPAN

> There is a Chinese saying which goes like this: "Tian Shi, Di Li, Ren He," meaning "Perfect Timing, Suitable Place, Cooperative People." NIU in the 1970s seems fit to this saying.
>
> —Dr. Kuo-Huang Han[1]

The NIU Steelband started with Al O'Connor, a native of Long Island, New York who loved music from an early age. O'Connor earned college degrees in music, focused on electronic and avant-garde music, taught in high school, and came to Northern Illinois University (hereafter NIU) to teach percussion. The program had no steelband, and only because of his desire and drive would one eventually exist. At the time O'Connor began his steelband endeavor there were almost no steelbands as part of university music programs in the United States; O'Connor had to create it all on his own.

If Al O'Connor had been an ethnomusicologist, things would have been different. That is, if O'Connor was not a musician, someone who on a cellular level wants to play and needs to make music, the NIU steelband program in its present form surely would not exist. Throughout academia there are many different philosophies of learning, some more theoretical and some more practical or application-based. Yet for O'Connor, there was only one way: the "learn by doing" philosophy. If he was going to teach percussionists, they were going to learn by playing. Likewise, if O'Connor was going to start a steelband, the band was going to learn by doing. Yet even O'Connor interpreted the latter more broadly than most, which is to say that at NIU not only do students learn steelpan by playing steelpan, but they also learn by arranging, gigging, touring, tuning, building, and living steelpan. If

O'Connor was going to have a steelband, this band was going to play top-notch arrangements, with the best-sounding steelpans played as well as possible. It is this drive to learn by doing that fundamentally shaped the NIU steelband program, and indeed O'Connor's entire career.

O'Connor had never touched or played a steelpan of any kind until after he finished college in 1967. This fact alone makes his lifelong journey with steelband all the more remarkable. He is, first and foremost, a musician, and beyond his skills as a pannist, O'Connor is an accomplished percussionist and performer. The pedigree of this would-be panman is typical for someone in academia in the United States. O'Connor earned a Bachelor of Science degree in education with a performer's certificate from SUNY–Fredonia in 1966. He immediately auditioned and was accepted as a graduate student to pursue a master's degree in percussion performance at the University of Illinois in Urbana, Illinois.

In the 1960s the University of Illinois housed one of the most progressive schools of music in the country, and O'Connor was excited to be a part of the creative atmosphere fostered on campus. He studied percussion with percussion professor Jack McKenzie, and it was here at the University of Illinois that O'Connor befriended a group of percussionists who would go on to become highly influential in the development of percussion programs in the United States. This group included the likes of Thomas Siwe (University of Illinois), Larry Snider (University of Akron), and Michael Udow (University of Michigan). McKenzie encouraged O'Connor and the other percussionists to work with living composers and composition students in order to foster relationships and create new works.

Beyond the confines of the traditional percussion department, O'Connor was drawn to the legendary Studio for Experimental Music at the University of Illinois. The program had gained a reputation of being on the cutting edge of electronic and computer music technology and composition since its inception in 1958. With his compositions "It's Gonna Rain" (1964) and "Come Out to Show Them" (1965), Steve Reich effectively invented the concept of phase music in the Studio for Experimental Music in Urbana, and the place was still pressing new boundaries on O'Connor's arrival in 1966. Remarkably, it was for a concert and recording session with members of the Studio for Experimental Music and the University of Illinois Contemporary Chamber Players that O'Connor was first introduced to the steelpan in the spring of 1967. The work was called "Underworld" and was written by University of Illinois composition professor Salvatore Martirano. The work was scored for four actors, four percussionists, two string basses, tenor sax, and two-channel tape. Each of the percussionists was allotted a multi-percussion setup that included a variety of instruments. And, serendipitously, O'Connor's multiple percussion setup called for him to play steelpan.

"Underworld" treated the steelpan as a found sound object, meaning that the instrument was not intended to be played in its traditional context. This made little difference as O'Connor had no idea about the steelpan's origins, Carnival, or Trinidad and Tobago. O'Connor's multiple percussion setup included several other bell-like instruments, and the steelpan was intended as one element of a metallic tonal fabric. At this point O'Connor had never seen a steelpan up close, let alone played one. He and his colleagues had to first locate a steelpan as the University of Illinois did not have one in their instrument collection. Someone from the University of Illinois rented steelpans from Frank's Drum Shop in Chicago (who had to source the instruments from New York), and O'Connor made the drive to downtown Chicago to pick up the instruments and bring them back to Champaign-Urbana.[2] With steelpan in hand, O'Connor was now charged with figuring out how to play the instrument as the composer Martirano was also clueless as to how one actually played the instrument—he simply loved its unique sound.[3] The score had no mallet indications, and the steelpan O'Connor rented came with no mallets. According to O'Connor, "I made about eight different kinds of sticks out of different types of material to try to get the thing to sound the way I wanted."[4] O'Connor's performance of "Underworld" was part of a later recitation of the work, and he was not one of the original performers for either the work's premiere or its professional recording, which was released in 1967 along with other new electro-acoustic works on the album *Electronic Music from the University of Illinois*.[5] Regardless, the experience of playing the new piece with the new instrument was a positive one for O'Connor, and despite playing the steelpan outside of its traditional context he was taken by the instrument. "Just the sound of it fascinated me."[6]

After graduating from the University of Illinois with a master's degree in percussion performance, O'Connor took a position at his high-school alma mater back in Long Island, New York: the Central Islip, New York, Public School District. Central Islip is located in the geographical middle of Long Island, and it was a familiar stomping ground for O'Connor and his wife Judith (also a musician and teacher). O'Connor was hired to teach percussion lessons and direct percussion ensembles in grades four through twelve throughout the entire school district. He had always set his sights on college teaching; however, without better prospects on the horizon, O'Connor took the position at Central Islip. The United States was deeply involved in the Vietnam War at this time and O'Connor's position as a teacher garnered him a draft exemption, and this exemption was extended when he moved on to DeKalb and NIU in 1968.[7]

O'Connor began his new post as a music teacher in Long Island during the summer of 1967 as he and his new wife, Judith, saved money to take a proper honeymoon. In August the newlyweds left for their delayed honeymoon, destined for the islands of St. Croix and St. Thomas in the US Virgin Islands. It was here that O'Connor saw real steelbands for the very first time (initially a small group of four or five, later a larger group of around fifteen players), and he was entranced by what he saw and heard. O'Connor and Judith honeymooned at the Grapetree Bay Resort in St. Croix and there saw Bill Bass and the Royal Tones steelband. In St. Thomas, the couple stayed at the Island Beachcomber Hotel where the Pott Steelers steelband entertained audiences daily.

As fate would have it, O'Connor had stumbled upon some of the most accomplished pannists in the Caribbean. Bill Bass has been one of the best-known pannists in the Virgin Islands for decades, recorded numerous albums, and performed countless professional engagements at various hotels and resorts.[8] The Pott Steelers[9] were led by Trinidadian Mike Alexander, an accomplished pannist in his own right, who came to New York with the Geoffrey Holder dance troupe in the early 1950s. Alexander also led the steelpan trio in the Broadway musical *House of Flowers* (1954), toured with Enid Mosier, and recorded with Harry Belafonte and Miriam Makeba.[10]

O'Connor was bitten by the "pan jumbie," what Trinidadians often call the spirit that guides the energy of the instrument and the culture that surrounds steelbands. A fascinated O'Connor said to himself, "I've got to have one of those things."[11] The bartender at the Grapetree Bay Resort in St. Croix was Trinidadian, and he and O'Connor became fast friends. After several days of O'Connor's persistent questions, the bartender connected him with another islander (who just so happened to be Trinidadian), who made a steelpan for O'Connor to take home. Within a few short days, O'Connor had a lead steelpan of much greater quality than the steelpans he had rented from the store in Chicago. Upon returning to Long Island, O'Connor began teaching himself to play steelpan and searching for music to perform. With no steelbands to speak of on Long Island, O'Connor focused his performing efforts on solo and mixed ensemble playing with jazz groups and choirs.

In the spring of 1968, O'Connor heard through an acquaintance that a full-time position for a percussion professor was soon opening at Northern Illinois University and that he should apply. He was eager to move on from secondary school teaching and excitedly applied for the position. O'Connor's skills as a performer and his experience with electronic and computer music won over the hiring committee, and he was hired for the position of Instructor of Percussion. In the late 1960s and early 1970s the idea of a full-time percussion professor was, in itself, a progressive act on the part of NIU, as most American universities regularly hired instructors for what were considered secondary instruments (percussion, guitar, jazz, etc.) on part-time basis.[12]

However, Northern Illinois saw an area ripe for growth, and O'Connor was charged with putting an emphasis on recruiting students and growing the department. With the business of recruiting students and building the department at hand, O'Connor's time was accounted for and then some. Steelpan would simply have to wait. In addition to teaching a growing number of percussion students, O'Connor (along with pianist J. B. Floyd) founded and managed the electronic and computer music studio at NIU and directed the mixed media group Electric Stereopticon, which included visual artists Norman Magden and Jeffery Pauli.[13] The group was awarded funding from the National Endowment of the Arts to commission four new works (from composers Morton Subotnik, Donald Erb, Larry Austin, and David Rosenboom) and performed throughout the United States, London, Canada, and Mexico.

As the years went by, O'Connor was consumed with his duties as director of percussion and slowly built the NIU percussion program into a regional power; however, he never forgot about the steelpan nor did his desire to start a steelband at NIU wane. His opportunity came in the form of a casual offer from one of his percussion students. By 1971 NIU had several partnerships with colleges and universities around the region, in which these smaller institutions would take advantage of the resources at the NIU School of Music. Their students could take lessons from NIU faculty in specific music disciplines—such as percussion—not commonly found at smaller music departments. One such partnership was with Beloit College in Beloit, Wisconsin, and several of their percussion students traveled the hour-and-fifteen-minute drive to DeKalb to study with O'Connor.

During December of 1971, Beloit College percussion student Jeff Rubin mentioned to O'Connor that he was going to Aruba for winter break and that he could buy steelpans

FIGURE 2.1. Al O'Connor Playing New steelpans (1970s)

for NIU if they were still interested. O'Connor pleaded with the chair of the NIU School of Music for an advance of $500, which he received shortly thereafter. What O'Connor did not know at the time was that despite being under the radar as a steelpan hotbed, other Caribbean islands such as Aruba and Antigua had long traditions of steelband excellence. Antiguan steelbands such as the Brute Force and Hell's Gate had been popular throughout the Caribbean as early as the 1950s,[14] and established bands such as the US Navy Steel Band preferred to purchase their lead steelpans from Antigua in the late 1950s and 1960s.[15] Come mid-March 1972, O'Connor received a phone call from Rubin indicating that the steelpans were going to arrive shortly at the airport in Chicago and that he needed to pick them up. After arguing with a customs agent about what these "things" actually were (they finally settled on calling them "bongo drums"), O'Connor secured the steelpans and brought them back to DeKalb.

O'Connor had the basics for his steelband, including a new collection of instruments and, it turned out, a bevy of interested students. However, he had no time to run the program with an ever-growing studio of percussion majors and ongoing duties with the electronic music studio. Complicating matters further, music and arrangements for steelbands were not readily available during the early 1970s, and O'Connor was responsible for finding and arranging all of the charts for the band. As such, the first NIU Steelband performance did not occur until the spring of 1974, at which the fledgling steelband performed three

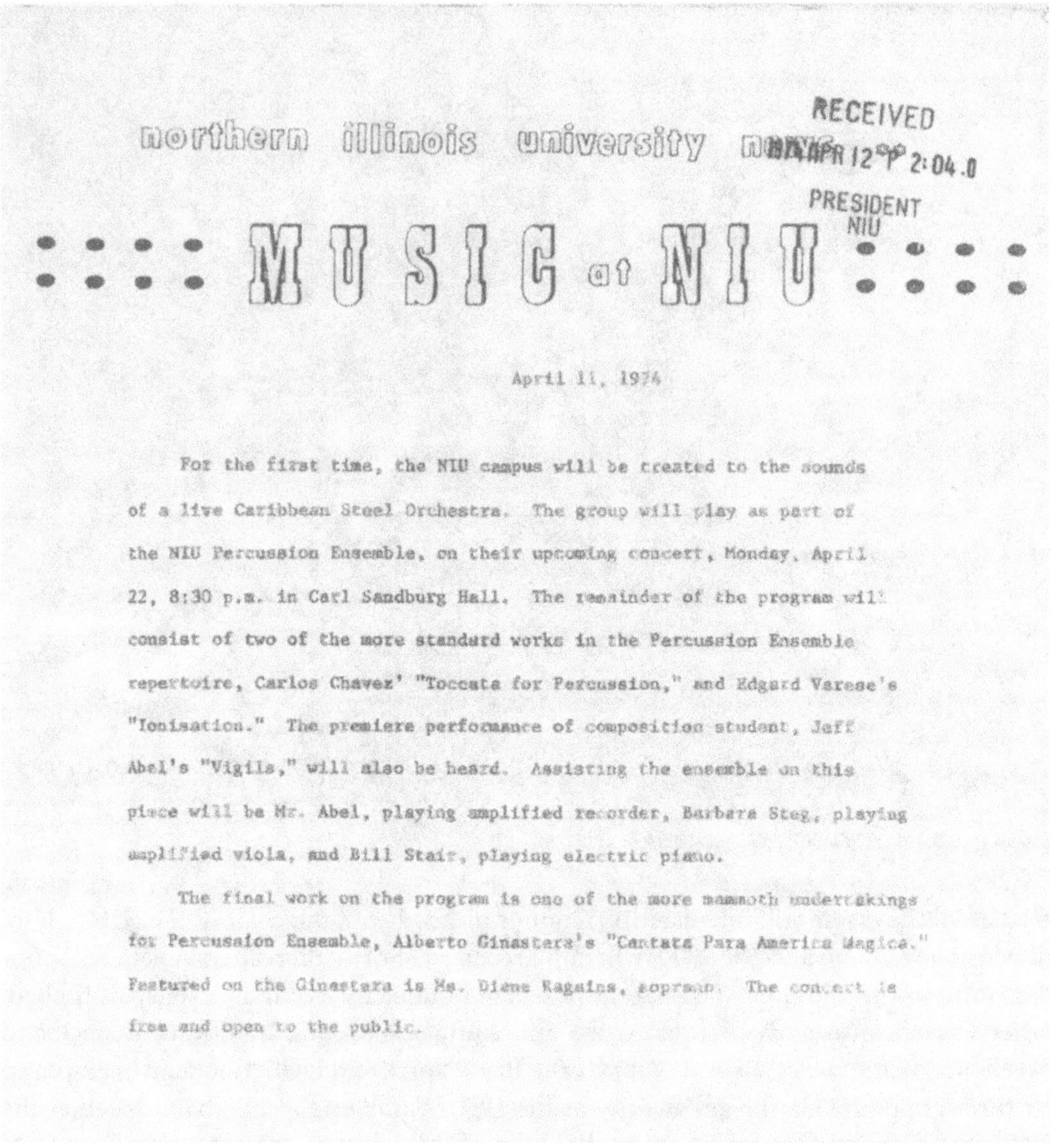

northern illinois university

RECEIVED APR 12 P 2:04.0 PRESIDENT NIU

:::: MUSIC at NIU ::::

April 11, 1974

For the first time, the NIU campus will be treated to the sounds of a live Caribbean Steel Orchestra. The group will play as part of the NIU Percussion Ensemble, on their upcoming concert, Monday, April 22, 8:30 p.m. in Carl Sandburg Hall. The remainder of the program will consist of two of the more standard works in the Percussion Ensemble repertoire, Carlos Chavez' "Toccata for Percussion," and Edgard Varese's "Ionisation." The premiere performance of composition student, Jeff Abel's "Vigils," will also be heard. Assisting the ensemble on this piece will be Mr. Abel, playing amplified recorder, Barbara Steg, playing amplified viola, and Bill Stair, playing electric piano.

The final work on the program is one of the more mammoth undertakings for Percussion Ensemble, Alberto Ginastera's "Cantata Para America Magica." Featured on the Ginastera is Ms. Diane Ragains, soprano. The concert is free and open to the public.

FIGURE 2.2. First NIU Steelband Concert Press Release (1974)

steelband pieces at the end of the percussion ensemble concert. Initially, steelband was simply an offshoot of the percussion ensemble, and O'Connor required his percussion ensemble members to play steelpan as a small part of the concert. However, the steelband was an immediate success and took on a life of its own. O'Connor began to add more and more steelband pieces to the percussion ensemble performances until, after a few short years, nearly half the percussion ensemble concerts consisted of steelband pieces. Non-percussion majors, too, began asking to join the band, instilling a newfound confidence in O'Connor that "after that, I knew we had something with this steelband thing."[16]

Beyond percussion ensemble concerts O'Connor found other venues on the NIU campus for his steelband to perform. Ethnomusicologist Kuo-Huang Han was initially hired at NIU in 1970 to teach Western music history. A Chinese music and Indonesian gamelan specialist, Han found the supportive NIU administration interested in expanding his teaching duties beyond the traditional Western canon, and they encouraged him to start world music ensembles. According to Han, in the spring of 1975, "I decided to do a world music concert that included many cultures; a student (Jeff Abel) and I cooked up the Latin title: "Musica Exotica" just for attraction. We didn't even know it was going to be the beginning of a series."[17] The marathon concerts were a cornucopia of world music, and the NIU Steelband performed along with the Americana, Chinese Lo-Ku, Sundanese Angklung, Thai Folk, West African Ensembles, Chinese Orchestra, Solo Chinese Cheng, Gamelan, Ragtimers Band, and Croatian Tamburitza Band.[18] The NIU Steelband would enjoy a modest run of performances on the Musica Exotica series throughout the 1970s. By 1980 the steelband had once again grown by leaps and bounds, and O'Connor made the decision to remove it from the Musica Exotica series. O'Connor and Professor Rich Holly, who taught marimba in the percussion department, decided to pair the steelband and the marimba ensemble together for concerts and titled the joint annual concert of the two groups "Rosewood-n-Steel."

From the beginning the NIU Steelband was a working band, performing around DeKalb and nearby communities as well as taking annual tours to the East Coast. O'Connor used his connections on Long Island as a means to book concerts at grade schools and community organizations during the semester overlap between the university and grade schools in New York. The typical grade school year runs approximately one month longer than the NIU school year, and upon the completion of spring semester at NIU, O'Connor would gather a group of interested steelband members, rehearse, load the vans, and head east. The East Coast concerts had a repertoire of approximately ten tunes, and the band would play thirty to forty concerts in the span of two or three weeks.

For the students the experience was paramount. Learning how to be a professional musician was a large goal of the tours, and dealing with cramped spaces, conflicting personalities, tired band mates, and trying performing conditions was par for the course. O'Connor also used these tours to vet elite performers who would later join another gigging band that played concerts around the Chicago area for the remainder of the summer. The elite steelband was a bit smaller than the touring band and usually had only five to seven players who were paid for playing gigs. This band filled most of July and August with concerts and rehearsals, and it was a great honor for an NIU steelband student to be chosen to be in the summer band.

On occasion O'Connor also recruited non-NIU students, many of whom attended Birch Creek Music Performance Center camps where O'Connor taught, to perform with his elite summertime gigging steelbands. One such non-NIU student, Michael Bento, recalled that in the summer of 1984, "I flew from Seattle to DeKalb to play in the NIU summer performing steel band [sic]. O'Connor agreed to let me play in this group after corresponding with him over the school year. This was a small ensemble of five or six players, and also a paying gig. O'Connor had booked community concerts all over the Chicago area, Sunday afternoon gigs at a local restaurant and other things, and he was going to pay us for each performance. Basically the whole month of July was booked. I

FIGURE 2.3. Setting up for Performance (circa 1976)

was thrilled, honored, and excited to get this opportunity to play steel band music and be in the Chicago area for the summer."[19]

Beginning in 1974 and throughout the early years of the NIU Steelband, O'Connor was careful not to use any NIU School of Music funds to support the steelband. O'Connor fashioned the band as self-sufficient, with performance and gig fees covering the cost of tuning instruments and purchasing new equipment. There were several reasons for seeking an independent funding source, and O'Connor weighed his options carefully. First, with a self-sufficient ensemble O'Connor was not subject to the standard array of budget fluctuations of the university. If the School of Music budget inexplicably tanked, the steelband program was unaffected and would still be able to operate. Second, O'Connor was keenly aware that beyond the initial $500 investment the NIU School of Music was unlikely to continually supply capital funds for the steelband program.

Tuning steelpans and replacing damaged or poor quality steelpans is a constant worry for any steelband leader, and O'Connor needed a steady revenue source to keep the band in working order. This was particularly important: in spite of starting the band with the Aruban steelpans in 1974, O'Connor was already replacing them with steelpans made by Grenadian George Richards as early as 1975.[20] Thirdly, the endless barrage of gigs at K–12 schools, churches, and community organizations allowed O'Connor the opportunity to spread the gospel of steelband while gaining significant exposure for the NIU music program. It was at one of these school concerts that O'Connor became completely convinced of the validity of considering steelpan a necessary tool for percussion majors making a career in music. Finally, O'Connor saw these gigs and performances as part of a larger pedagogical tool and was convinced that School of Music administration and perspective students could plainly see that "steelband makes money and is not a money pit for the school. It equips these students to the life of a professional musician just the same way as the jazz band would."[21] From the administration's point of view, this was extra work for O'Connor, beyond his required contracted load, and if he wanted to have a steelband that was fine with them as long as it did not cost the university any money.

The students who came through the NIU program found a use for their talents. With more and more of his percussion graduates being asked to start or run steelband programs at their new respective graduate schools or school teaching jobs, O'Connor was further convinced of the worth of the NIU steelband program as a tool for his percussion graduates. NIU did not officially institute a degree in steelpan performance until 2007; however, from day one O'Connor was supportive of any student who wanted to pursue steelpan seriously, and several steelpan-loving individuals earned degrees in percussion with a primary focus on steelpan. Several early members of the NIU Steelband and those affiliated with the program went on to faculty positions at colleges and universities throughout North America, including coauthor Jeannine Remy (University of the West Indies–St. Augustine, Trinidad and Tobago), Shannon Dudley (University of Washington), Harold Headley (University of the West Indies–St. Augustine, Trinidad and Tobago) and several others discussed in the later chapters of this book.

CHAPTER 3

FROM HUMMINGBIRD TO HUSKY

Cliff Alexis Arrives at Northern Illinois University

> Mr. George Richards had built a set of steel drums for me in the summer of 1977. I brought him to DeKalb several times in 1977 and 1978 to re-tune the instruments as they would lose their true pitch almost every six months. It became obvious to me that if I were ever going to develop a viable steelband program at NIU, I would have to learn to re-tune the drums we had in our possession.
>
> —Al O'Connor (1979)[1]

By 1980 O'Connor was facing the harsh reality that maintaining steelpans in good working order was, in itself, practically a full-time job. Keeping the NIU Steelband's instruments in top shape was no small task, and he was keenly aware that a steelpan was like a piano and that in order to keep the instruments sounding their best, an in-house tuner would be necessary. The idea of having an in-house tuner for piano and other instruments is standard practice in university music programs, professional orchestras, and music organizations throughout the United States and the world. Considering that the NIU School of Music has well in excess of 125 pianos, each requiring at least two tunings per year, one can see the logistics and necessity of having a piano tuner. The only problem for O'Connor and the NIU Steelband's quest for a permanent steelpan tuner, of course, was that the NIU School of Music was not yet ready to commit funding to such a position, nor was a qualified tuner available for hire.

Further, despite the steady stream of income generated by the NIU Steelband's performances, O'Connor's steelpan budget was woefully inadequate to fund a full-time steelpan tuner position on its own—if such a person could even be found. Without better options on the horizon, O'Connor took it upon himself to learn the art of tuning steelpans. As he would soon come to realize, this was a far from simple task, but one that he nonetheless undertook.

Since acquiring the first instruments for the band in 1972, O'Connor had made only minimal efforts to learn the art of tuning steelpan on his own; however, starting in 1978 and continuing for the next couple of years, he took short sabbatical leaves of two to three weeks to study steelpan building and tuning with George Richards in Orlando, Florida. A native of the Caribbean island of Grenada, Richards was an experienced steelpan builder and tuner. When not tuning steelpans across the United States, Richards led and maintained the Grenadian National Steel Band in Grenada. During his studies with Richards, O'Connor spent two weeks at a time working with the master tuner before returning to DeKalb to practice his methods. After much work, sweat, and consternation O'Connor successfully fashioned himself one instrument, a set of cello steelpans. This small triumph was rewarding no doubt, but it also opened O'Connor's eyes to the bigger issue of time management. "I'm never going to learn to do this myself; it'll kill me!" he reasoned.[2] In his sabbatical report of 1980, O'Connor commented, "My attempts to learn tuning may earn plaudits from various academics and respect from West Indians. But for me, it pointed to the fact that I began to understand how little I actually knew about tuning pan."[3] The gravity of the situation was setting in, and O'Connor slowly realized that one needs to apprentice for several years in order to properly learn the art of steelpan tuning and building—years that O'Connor did not have to devote to the craft.

O'Connor was in a bind. On one hand, he wanted to have a viable steelband program on par with any in Trinidad. O'Connor was a performer first and foremost, and he wanted a top-notch steelband that sounded its best each and every day. On the other hand, he was faced with the problem of somehow acquiring an in-house tuner, as it was abundantly clear that he himself would not fit the bill and that the steelpans needed constant attention, not the occasional—sometimes yearly—tunings that have for better or worse become common practice among American steelbands.

Unfortunately for O'Connor, the NIU Steelband was, at the time, one of a kind. There were no other institutions in the United States with successful steelband programs for O'Connor to use as a model. If not a university music program, then could O'Connor perhaps look to another kind of institution for help? In the late 1970s the only institutionally based full-time steelband in the United States was the US Navy Steel Band stationed in New Orleans. O'Connor had seen the US Navy Steel Band in concert on tour in Crystal Lake, Illinois, in 1975 and was greatly inspired by the musicianship and wonderful sound of the band. According to O'Connor, "Nobody sounded as good as this band back then."[4] The US Navy Steel Band, with 12–16 players, was rather small in comparison to Trinidadian Panorama-style counterparts with 40–100 players, but they were renowned for having the best-sounding steelpans in the United States and, some have argued, the world.[5] Now, three years removed from seeing the US Navy Steel Band, O'Connor speculated as to who tuned and built steelpans for them. As it turned out, at the time, the US Navy Steel Band was tuned by a Trinidadian named Cliff Alexis who happened to live in St. Paul, Minnesota, only a half-day drive from DeKalb.

O'Connor soon learned that Cliff Alexis was a top-notch tuner and, equally as important for O'Connor, had the appropriate immigration papers to work in the United States. O'Connor knew that if he was ever going to hire Alexis (or anyone else) at NIU, the master tuner would need the requisite steelpan skills *and* a green card, assuming this person was a Caribbean national. Yet, how Alexis eventually arrived at NIU after being wooed by O'Connor is another story, one that began long ago in Trinidad, far removed from the snow and ice of St. Paul and the rolling cornfields of DeKalb.

Enter Cliff Alexis

Clifford Pierre (he would later change his last name to Alexis after his mother's surname) was born January 15, 1937, in Port of Spain, Trinidad. The oldest of five siblings, Alexis grew up in a neighborhood called Clifton Hill—sometimes referred to as one of several geographical neighborhoods situated "Behind the Bridge"—on the southeast side of the Trinidadian capital city of Port of Spain. Clifton Hill was one of the poor neighborhoods at the edge of downtown Port of Spain, and young Alexis was exposed to the good and bad of urban life, everything the community had to offer. As a boy, Alexis attended Rosary Boys School and Belmont Intermediate School. Despite being a good student, he had an independent streak and did not always get along with the nuns and their "rules."

Alexis's early childhood was marked with tragedy when his mother died during childbirth in 1942. The event left Alexis in the care of his father at the age of five. His father would soon remarry, though Alexis never connected emotionally with his stepmother. To complicate matters further, Alexis's father died in a tragic factory accident in late December of 1948, making Alexis an orphan at the age of eleven. He would go on to live with his aunt in the middle-class Port of Spain suburb Diego Martin until adulthood. Without the supervision of his parents, Alexis, like many Trinidadian youth, spent his days hanging around the panyards.

Beginning at the age of eight, Alexis snuck into the panyard of the Clifton Hill–based Hill 60 steelband whenever he got the chance. Following his relocation to Diego Martin, Alexis would regularly slip away from the watchful eyes of his aunt and make his way to Woodbrook in order to visit the panyard of the Hit Paraders steelband and later the legendary Invaders Steel Orchestra. Alexis attributes his prodigious musical aptitude to his mother and father, who were both musical, and he also had an uncle who was in the local police band. However, it was Alexis's own inner curiosity and precociousness as a child that sparked his musical interest.

The 1940s and 1950s was a time of great development in the relatively insular world of Trinidadian steelbands. Advancements in tuning, building, and arranging were happening at breakneck pace as steelbands competed against each other for glory, pride, and even a little money. The experimental stage of the steelpan's development as an instrument family was in full bloom, and individual builders and tuners attempted to solve many of the steelpans' idiosyncrasies.[6] The lack of uniformity among steelpan builders resulted in an explosion of creativity, and it was here, in this world of innovation, that Alexis developed his pioneering spirit. At Hill 60, Alexis relished the opportunity to learn from such legendary panmen as Patcheye, Andrew "Pan" De La Bastide, and Randolph "Ronny" Babb. According to Alexis, "The panyard is a university, and class is always in session!"[7]

At the Hit Paraders steelband, Alexis befriended bandleader Gerard Fernandez and became a regular in the panyard. It was with the Hit Paraders steelband that Alexis played his first Carnival in 1952 at age fifteen. The social stigma of associating with panmen was in full force in the early 1950s, and Alexis specifically chose the Hit Paraders steelband in Woodbrook with the thought of hiding his involvement from his family. Alexis explained, "A decent person would not have been caught with steeldrum players, except during Carnival." Young and impressionable, Alexis was not interested in the turf warfare waged by the so-called "bad johns" found in Port of Spain's tight-knit neighborhoods.[8] Rather, he was focused on learning steelpan, commenting, "I had to hang out with some pretty shady characters, but they had the skills."[9]

Alexis never received formal musical training; however, there is a Trinidadian credo that claims "the panyard *is* the university," and his unofficial apprenticeship in the panyards slowly filled this gap in formal training. His continued pursuit of knowledge and musical understanding separate Alexis from other panman; he is a musician versus someone who "beats" steelpan. Alexis remembers being chased out of the Invaders panyard by Ellie Mannette, who said, "All you Hit Paraders doh come here ... no more all you does do is take the tune and carry it down Anna Street."[10] Never satisfied, Alexis was pushing to know more. He is still, to this day, pushing to learn more.

Over the course of a few short years, Alexis moved on from the Hit Paraders steelband to play in the Tripoli steelband in the St. James neighborhood, then to the Stereophonics steelband of Petit Valley and the Joyland steelband of Laventille. Now in his early twenties, Alexis began arranging music for steelbands, and the Stereophonics steelband was the first band to perform one of his arrangements. Throughout all of this, Alexis was playing with the Invaders Steel Orchestra in Woodbrook. Alexis often refers to his time with the Invaders Steel Orchestra and its many pioneering panmen as his "real education." According to Alexis, "In Invaders, I was standing next to people like Errol Zephyrine and Emmanuel "Cobo Jack" Riley, who was the first real improviser on pan."[11] Led by steelpan legend Ellie Mannette, the Invaders Steel Orchestra drew the best talent from the area, and oftentimes other bands would send scouts to the Invaders panyard to look for arrangers.[12] This is how Alexis was chosen to arrange for both the Stereophonics steelband and the Joylanders steelband. Alexis, like many young panmen, was overjoyed with the exposure and hipness of playing in the Invaders Steel Orchestra during this era. It earned him respect and

FIGURE 3.1. Trinidad and Tobago National Steel Orchestra (1964). Cliff Alexis is in bottom row, third from left.

admiration among the steelpan aficionados. Yet, he was also there to learn from the masters. Beyond Mannette, several other legendary panmen frequented the Invaders panyard, and Alexis took the opportunity to soak in everything he could from each of them.

Despite never having a single formal music lesson of any kind, by 1964 the reputation of Alexis's accomplishments as an arranger and skill as a player had grown enough for him to be selected as a member of the National Steelband Orchestra of Trinidad and Tobago—an all-star band sponsored by the Trinidad and Tobago Steelbandsmen Association (the precursor to Pan Trinbago).[13] The band performed around Trinidad and Tobago for important government and cultural events and was comprised of the best players from throughout the country. The National Steelband Orchestra of Trinidad and Tobago also embarked on several international tours, and twenty-two men were chosen for a prestigious performance in Michigan, only the best of the best; Alexis joined Edwin Pouchet, Hugh Borde, Lennox "Bobby" Mohammad, and several other top panmen from across the island. Though originally planned as a short, weekend-long tour, the band spent the better part of 1964 touring the United States.[14] Despite turning into a tour of Michigan and the American Southwest, the primary purpose for the National Steelband Orchestra of Trinidad and Tobago's coming to the United States was to perform at the Moral Re-Armament Conference in Mackinaw Island, Michigan. The engagement was arranged by the president of the Trinidad and Tobago Steelbandsmen Association, George Goddard, and officials from the Moral Re-Armament organization.

The Moral Re-Armament movement is an international network of people of all faiths and backgrounds. The faith-based movement was a call to arms, and its core principle was that changing the world starts with seeking change in one's self. The organization encouraged its members to actively participate in political and social issues. The idealism and self-reliance of the Moral Re-Armament movement appealed to many African, Asian, and Caribbean nations seeking independence in the early 1960s. Trinidadians, in particular, embraced the Moral Re-Armament movement and saw its idealism as closely aligned with struggles for independence from Great Britain.[15]

To say that the National Steel Orchestra was received well at the Moral Re-Armament Conference in Michigan would be putting it lightly. The orchestra was a smash success, and its initial two-week engagement for the conference was extended into an unplanned two-month stay in the United States. Attendees of the Moral Re-Armament Conference were captivated by the music and enthusiasm of the National Steel Orchestra. Band member Edwin Pouchet enthusiastically told the *Trinidad Guardian*, "We are willing to play anywhere the Moral Re-Armament suggests for they know our music is as dynamic as their ideologies."[16] The leaders of the Moral Re-Armament took them up on the offer and immediately set in motion plans to bus the National Steel Orchestra to Harlem to sooth racial tensions.[17]

This leg of the trip never materialized, but the band did start a tour to a number of cities. In Michigan, the band performed in the sister cities of St. Ignatius and Mackinaw City near the Moral Re-Armament grounds on Mackinaw Island. Other performances in Michigan included cities such as Harbor Springs, Petoskey, and Charlevoix as the band made its way east. They performed in Wheeling, West Virginia, before heading west. In Oklahoma City, Oklahoma, the band performed a special concert in the rotunda of the governor's house. The band planned a special event in a small town 200 miles south of Denver because of the town's name: Trinidad, Colorado. Indeed, the National Steelband Orchestra of Trinidad and Tobago performed there on August 31 in honor of Trinidad and Tobago's independence day. Further west, the band was treated to a hero's welcome in Santa Fe, New Mexico, where it appeared on local television and performed in the rotunda of the New Mexico capital building.[18] Following their trip to Santa Fe, the visas of the many of the individual steel orchestra members expired, and the National Steel Orchestra returned home to Trinidad and Tobago. For the twenty-seven-year-old Alexis, the experience was eye-opening and convinced him that steelpan could take him places far beyond the island shores of Trinidad and Tobago.

Upon returning from the National Steel Orchestra tour, Alexis became restless and in 1965 moved to New York. There he joined the steelband BWIA Sunjets as a pannist/arranger and began performing in the greater New York City area. Despite returning to Trinidad for Carnival and other assorted brief visits, Alexis has since lived exclusively in the United States. While in New York, he relied on an old friend from Trinidad, Patrick Arnold, to tune the steelpans for the BWIA Sunjets. Alexis knew the theory of tuning from his days in the panyards of Trinidad, but it was Arnold who encouraged Alexis to learn the art of tuning, and Alexis obliged: "I knew the whole theory of tuning, but not the practicum [*sic*]."¹⁹ Arnold's encouragement and generosity greatly impacted Alexis. "He [Arnold] is one of the persons I would give anything to or do anything for."²⁰ Alexis's time with the BWIA Sunjets lasted for a few very productive years in which he led and arranged for the band, including performances at Carnegie Hall and the Macy's Thanksgiving Day Parade.

At this time, the most successful steelband from Trinidad in America was the Trinidad Tripoli steelband led by Hugh Borde. The band had gone to Expo 67 in Montreal to perform, where famed pianist and entertainer Liberace noticed and hired them as his opening act. For the next few years the band crisscrossed America and appeared on a series of high-profile shows with Liberace. Visa problems and internal tensions led to Borde having a band name and a contract, but few players. Borde knew Alexis from back in Trinidad and hired him to join the band for a tour in the fall of 1967. Liberace's personnel director was impressed with Alexis's playing, arrangements, and bandleader skills, and he encouraged the panman to form another band to be promoted along with the Trinidad Tripoli steelband. The result of this collaboration was a band called Cliff Alexis and the Trinidad Troubadours steelband. This new band again took Alexis across the United States performing from coast to coast. The longevity of this band was much greater than anything Alexis had previously experienced and kept him performing almost continuously from 1967 to 1972. In 1972 Alexis needed a break from the life of constant touring and decided to move to St. Paul, Minnesota, where his then wife had family. Alexis liked the city of St. Paul; however, he needed to earn an income, which meant that he also had to find work in a place without a steelband scene.

The same national sentiments in American education that embraced multiculturalism and world cultures and that guided the O'Connor's experimentation of steelband at NIU were also in play for Alexis, and he was able to quickly parlay his skills as a panmen into a job at St. Paul Central High School teaching steelpan. The school had had no such program prior to Alexis's arrival, and he was tasked with teaching inner-city kids steelpan as part of a curricular school music program that also included beginner, intermediate, and advanced steelbands five days a week. The faculty at St. Paul Central High School auditioned Alexis, despite his lack of formal music education, by observing him work with the students. A natural teacher, Alexis charmed everyone with his ability to relate to even the toughest of disadvantaged students. He understood their background and their talent and never doubted their ability to create music. Alexis had secured a job, but he had little resources with which to work. The school superintendent promised Alexis nothing: no funding and no promise that the program would continue beyond a trial period. Alexis boldly asserted to the superintendent that he could supply the steelpans and maintain the instruments from scratch. In essence, he committed to building the steelpans, tuning them, creating the arrangements, teaching the students to play an instrument they had never seen, and leading the band as the school did not have the budget to purchase ready-made steelpans or sheet music and arrangements.

At this point in his life, Alexis was an experienced pannist, but he was not a builder and was incapable of building a set of steelpans on his own. Teaching in Minnesota inspired Alexis and made him want to become a builder and tuner. Beyond this desire, however, there were no tuners in the area. Alexis again turned to Trinidadian Patrick Arnold, his friend from the Sunjets steelband in New York, to build the first set of steelpans for St. Paul Central. Ultimately, Alexis apprenticed to Patrick Arnold as a steelpan builder/tuner. In addition to his work studying with Patrick Arnold (and his observations as a young man of Ellie Mannette in the Invaders panyard), Alexis further honed his tuning abilities by undertaking advanced studies in music and acoustics. Alexis used every opportunity to explore everything he could about the subject, including taking a twelve-week course in piano tuning at the University of Minnesota and reading books on instrument tuning. Leaving no stone unturned, he would later consult with various marimba tuners and organ tuners, and even went to a harp convention to study tuning. His interest in instrument tuning and acoustics continued throughout his years at NIU.[21]

Alexis's perseverance and hard work paid off, and soon he had instruments that he could tune. Meanwhile, he clicked with the students he taught, and the program in St. Paul was a success, earning accolades from administration and state-wide education and arts organizations in Minnesota. Alexis was recognized with the 1983 and 1984 "Minnesota Black Musician of the Year" award. Through his continued work in St. Paul, Alexis became a renowned tuner and builder of steelpans among education and academic circles, which further landed him on the short list of tuners/builders used by the US Navy Steel Band during the mid-1970s, where his quality instruments came to Al O'Connor's attention.

FIGURE 3.2. Cliff Alexis working at St. Paul Central High School (1970s)

Al O'Connor first reached out to Alexis in 1980 in search of help in acquiring new steelpans and tuning old ones. The two men became instant friends; as O'Connor recalled, "The two of us just clicked."[22] O'Connor knew that Alexis's steelpans were of the highest quality and that the gifted panman was improving his tuning skills with each new instrument; however, O'Connor became equally impressed with the panman's sharp wit, musical ability and intellect. O'Connor would later comment, "It was obvious to me that the guy was a musical genius, no matter what amount of formal musical training he may have had."[23]

For his part Alexis was happy to make steelpans for O'Connor and NIU. But from the beginning O'Connor wanted more, hoping to persuade Alexis to move to DeKalb and be the band's full-time builder of new instruments and tuner. However, Alexis had a steady job in St. Paul; he cared deeply for his students and was involved in mentoring several gifted individuals, including a group of students who formed the nationally successful soul/R&B band Mint Condition (whose 1992 hit "Breakin' My Heart (Pretty Brown Eyes)" rose to number six on the Billboard Hot 100). Alexis himself was also busy performing and arranging with two bands—the reggae/pop band, Shangoya, and a small steelband made up of his students, The Cliff Alexis Experience, that performed throughout the greater Twin Cities area.[24] Once he was fully aware of the extent to which Alexis was involved in the Twin Cities music scene, O'Connor knew that persuading him to come to NIU would be a tall order, and he set about the process of trying to convince Alexis to move to DeKalb. This mission took the better part of five years.

Initially, Alexis was skeptical of the NIU Steelband. For a faculty recital in the spring of 1980, O'Connor had transcribed an Andy Narell piece written for steelpan and piano and arranged it for a small multi-voice steelband ensemble. It was this recording that made clear to Alexis how seriously O'Connor took steelpan.

> I played him [Alexis] a tape of the performance, and I could tell he was really blown away. All he could talk about is how great the pan sounded. So that was pretty much the thing that convinced him that I was serious about this. He would go to other schools and would still be thinking that the instrument was part of their percussion program and many times they wouldn't be involved in playing it. They would turn it over to a grad assistant or something and then take all the credit. He could see I was performing. I knew about the instrument, and I was really trying to learn more.[25]

O'Connor knew that he would need to secure a permanent position for Alexis if he were to lure him from St. Paul to NIU. A visiting professor or similar position would not work as it would always be subject to the budget ax, and gigging by the NIU Steelband would never be enough to cover the cost of a full-time hire. O'Connor began strategizing with colleagues at NIU to create a position there that would meet the university's desires for a tuner and Alexis's needs for income, health insurance, and security.

Meanwhile, O'Connor set about earning Alexis's trust by first purchasing a steady stream of instruments. The original sets of steelpans that O'Connor had acquired from Aruba in 1972, now over a decade old, were in poor shape, and those steelpans added via the work

FIGURE 3.3. NIU Steelband playing Cliff Alexis made steelpans (circa early 1980s)

of Grenadian George Richards could not approach the quality of the steelpans crafted by Alexis. Slowly, O'Connor began buying steelpans from Alexis and replacing the preexisting sets at NIU one at a time as money became available. O'Connor and Alexis would each drive halfway between DeKalb and St. Paul and meet for lunch (somewhere near Janesville, Wisconsin) to exchange steelpans.

Over the course of three years, these roadside exchanges allowed O'Connor the opportunity to communicate to Alexis how serious he was about steelband as an art form, as well as his plans for outfitting the entire NIU steelband with Alexis's steelpans. In 1984, O'Connor took another one-semester sabbatical in which he regularly drove to St. Paul every two weeks in order to study tuning and building with Alexis. This attempt at learning the art of making steelpans greatly impressed Alexis; O'Connor saw these tuning sessions as his opportunity to convince Alexis to come to NIU. The turning point came in the summer of 1984 when O'Connor and Alexis were both guest artists at a steelpan workshop at the University of Akron. Working together, the pair made a great team (a point that became obvious to both men), and they began to believe that the partnership could work on a more formal and permanent level. In the spring of 1985, O'Connor brought the NIU Steelband to River Falls, Wisconsin (thirty miles from St. Paul), for a series of concerts. He invited Alexis to come to the concerts and to tune the band. At this point Alexis had only heard the NIU Steelband on record, and he was blown away hearing the NIU Steelband live. He finally agreed to move to DeKalb once the steelpan tuner/builder position was secured.[26]

At the same time, O'Connor was promoted to assistant chair of the School of Music at NIU. This was a time of great transition as the NIU "Department of Music" was becoming a stand-alone "School of Music" with greater degree-granting capabilities. Furthermore, the School of Music was getting a new music building, and O'Connor was put in charge of equipping the building with furnishings and fixtures. The new building was greatly needed by the percussion department, which was housed off campus in a university-owned house at the time.

> You see, when I [O'Connor] came here [1968] the music building was shared with art and theatre in this teeny little place on the outside of campus ... I had moved the percussion program out of that place [into a house the university owned]. We had the Black Earth percussion group in the basement, the steelband was in the kitchen, percussion practice rooms and the ensemble were in the bedrooms and living room.[27]

With a workload now partially devoted to administration, O'Connor took the opportunity to shift resources and create a half-time position for Alexis as an "instrumental technician/steel drum" in the service branch of NIU. The state of Illinois government employee service, which includes university employees, had one of the strongest unions in the country during the 1980s. O'Connor knew that once Alexis was hired and credentialed by the state government he would have the job security he so desired.

And so, after years of work on O'Connor's part, the matter was settled. Alexis moved to DeKalb in the late spring of 1985 and began immediately working on steelpans in an office on the second floor of the NIU music building—the same office that he still uses to this day. For the first month of the fall semester in August, things progressed smoothly, and Alexis settled into his new role. He was to report to his supervisor (O'Connor) and maintain the growing number of steelpans housed at NIU. All that needed to be done was for O'Connor to have Alexis register with human resources, and the position would be set. Yet trouble arose immediately. During the 1980s the state government of Illinois was in the midst of a vicious budget gridlock, and the civil service was subject to a hiring freeze.[28] O'Connor brought Alexis to NIU's human resources department and said, "Hire him." He was told, "First he has to take and pass the qualifying test, and then you have to advertise the position publicly."[29] It came as quite a shock to both men that Alexis, like anyone else, needed to pass the civil-service exam in order to retain his technical position—even one as specialized as steelpan tuner.

But what exam would he take? Surely, there was no exam for a steelpan tuner in the Illinois civil service handbook. After much deliberation by local and state government officials, it was decided that Alexis would sit for the "piano tuner" exam.[30] The exam was to take six hours and cover all aspects of piano tuning, acoustics, and cursory-level music theory. Alexis finished the exam after four hours, and his exam was graded immediately.

He had managed to score in the 80th percentile, well beyond the 60th percentile needed to pass the exam. The only thing separating him from a permanent position at NIU was a ninety-day probationary period. Alexis called O'Connor to break the news:

> Cliff called me and said, "Sorry, boss, but I failed the test." I panicked, and feeling terrible about the whole situation, told him something like "Don't worry, we'll see if you can retake the test or something," at which point he burst into laughter and said, "Relax man, I passed, I passed."[31]

A day or two later the two men sat down and wrote the job qualifications in a way that only Alexis could satisfy, advertised it in the two smallest newspapers in the two most obscure places in Illinois, and after ninety days the permanent half-time position was set. And so Cliff Alexis, a man of many talents, became "Cliff Alexis—Instrument Repair Technician 2," and the NIU Steelband had its steelpan builder/tuner for the next three decades.

CHAPTER 4

THE O'CONNOR/ALEXIS ERA AND THE NIU/BIRCH CREEK CONNECTION

> The advances this organization has made through this academic year [1985] with his [Alexis's] help have been phenomenal. The University has been well publicized in Trinidad (where steel drums were invented) as a place that is fostering the development of the instrument at a faster pace than in its country of origin.. It would be a tragedy if he had to leave DeKalb because we could not match our competitors. I am urgently requesting your support in attempting to create a position for him that would give him access to our health coverage and a moderate stipend for his assistance to the organization. An offer of this type would be enough to keep him, his heart is at NIU.
>
> —Al O'Connor (1986)[1]

As of the fall of 1985, Alexis was a permanent member of the NIU School of Music staff. While his primary raison d'être was the instruments, both tuning and building new steelpans, he slowly became much more for the band. However, he was initially stymied by the fact that he did not have a full-time job. Together O'Connor and Alexis began plotting a new direction for the NIU Steelband and new roles for Cliff to play. As Instrument Repair Technician 2, Alexis reported directly to O'Connor for matters of oversight, administration, and promotion. As such, O'Connor made his best effort to always give Alexis superior ratings on his employee evaluations, which over time would incrementally boost his pay and change his job classification. Yet, Alexis's position remained half-time throughout the academic year 1985–86. In an effort to make good on his promise of full-time work, O'Connor pleaded with the NIU administration to retain Alexis by any means necessary.

School of Music Chair Dr. Donald Funes and Dean of the College of Visual and Performing Arts Stanley Madeja were sympathetic to O'Connor's request, but the funds were not readily available.

O'Connor knew he had to act fast, as word of Alexis's success at NIU had quickly spread throughout the ranks of percussion professors nationwide, and many were interested in starting steelband programs, but lacked the expertise. The idea of having Alexis tune and build steelpans in-house at their respective home institutions was tantalizing, and when Professor Gary Cook made Alexis a formal offer to join the staff at the University of Arizona in the early winter of 1985, O'Connor's search for funds at NIU took on a fever pitch.[2] With his recent two-year assignment to oversee the facilities installation (chairs, tables, fixtures, and the like) in the new NIU School of Music building, O'Connor saw just the opportunity he was looking for and lobbied once again for support. This time O'Connor used Alexis in his new role as recruiter, and the diversity his hire brought to the faculty and student population of NIU, as the ultimate bargaining chip. In a memo to Dean Madeja, O'Connor wrote "He [Alexis] has already recruited several minority students for the department from his former school and I have received communications from potential students around the U.S. and even the West Indies who are interested in attending NIU because of his presence here."[3]

O'Connor's urgent call for action was successful, and Alexis was appointed Adjunct Lecturer of Music by the NIU board of regents on a contract for two years at half-time. This new position of lecturer was to be held in addition to Alexis's position as Instrument Repair Technician 2, and would require him to direct the NIU Steelband in O'Connor's absence. In combining the two half-time positions, O'Connor had succeeded in creating the full-time position that he had promised. Alexis informed the St. Paul school district that his one-year leave of absence would become permanent and officially resigned his position in the spring of 1986.

Of course, the irony of Alexis's new position as adjunct lecturer was that from the time he arrived on campus at NIU, Alexis assumed the role of steelpan tuner in a manner much more conducive to the Trinidadian style of doing things. That is, despite being hired to tune and build steelpans Alexis had, from day one, actively participated in the direction of the NIU Steelband. He led the NIU Steelband in rehearsals, arranged new pieces for the band, wrote new pieces for the band, and in the summer of 1985 formed a small six- or seven-person gigging steelband that performed throughout the greater Chicagoland area. Alexis brought two experienced students (Paulette Frazier and Twyla Cole) with him from St. Paul to NIU in order to get the band established. Alexis also brought a number of his compositions from the bands he had in Minnesota, and the "little band" as it was called was up and running in short order. O'Connor played double tenor, and Alexis double second. Other members included Mike Shepherd, Doug Dale, Paulette Frazier, and Paul Ross on drum set. Ross has vivid memories of this incredible experience, which included regular gigs and endless rehearsals: "It was smoking. . . . [It] was great because we were playing so much."[4]

FIGURE 4.1. "Little Band" Steelband Promotional Card (early 1980s)

O'Connor's absence was not really an absence per se as he still played in the band; however, Alexis led/directed the steelband, resuming a position he knew well from his earlier career in Trinidad and New York. From the onset of Alexis's arrival at NIU, O'Connor considered him a co-director of the NIU steelband program. The two men have different strengths, and the first few years of the partnership was a period of feeling things out and establishing clearly defined individual roles. Alexis was obviously going to tune and build steelpans, and O'Connor's administrative talents suggested that he was going to oversee student recitals, academic advising, etc. Yet, both Alexis and O'Connor discovered new talents in one another as a result of their partnership, and their individual roles continued to develop over time.

Alexis and O'Connor encouraged and pushed the artistic development of the other as colleagues, as well as pushing their students. For example, O'Connor saw that spending fifteen years in St. Paul teaching beginning-level middle- and high-school students had stagnated Alexis's arranging skills, and he encouraged Alexis to begin arranging more challenging music for the NIU Steelband from the very first days of his arrival in DeKalb.

Alexis, on the other hand, pushed O'Connor to create (and the university offer) an official degree program in steelpan at NIU. When he arrived in 1985 the current system of letting pannists earn degrees in percussion by focusing on steelpan was not, in his opinion, enough, and he lobbied O'Connor from day one to push toward an official degree program, something not available elsewhere in the United States.

The addition of Alexis also allowed O'Connor to focus on developing his role as an administrator. In 1983, O'Connor was promoted to assistant chair of the NIU School of Music, the first in a string of promotions that would eventually transition him from the ranks of faculty to that of administration. He would retire in 2002 as the Associate Dean of the College of Visual and Performance Arts at NIU. Yet, it was Alexis's arrival in 1985 that sparked O'Connor's transition to administration in earnest. After ceding many of his teaching duties to Alexis, O'Connor instead focused on the steelband budget and administrative duties and, from 1990–2002 the various tours the band took around the globe, which required significant effort in securing grants and funding.

The synergy between the two men was best on display in their daily work rehearsing the NIU Steelband. Alexis had a special set of skills that O'Connor knew would fill a void in traditional music education. He would later tell the *City Sun* newspaper, "It was my intention from the beginning to think of steel drums not as a novelty, but to have people learn the music of where they came from. Alexis has tremendous musical abilities in areas most students don't experience."[5]

Prior to Alexis's arrival, O'Connor had, with the exception of a few gifted students and guest artists, created all the arrangements for the NIU Steelband. He was accustomed to leading the rehearsals, which met five days a week for one hour. However, with the arrival of Alexis, O'Connor felt himself a bit of an interloper, and even more, he had a great admiration for Alexis's abilities. With few exceptions, O'Connor rather quickly deferred most of the directing of the NIU Steelband to Alexis. This meant that Alexis was now going to rehearse the NIU Steelband in calypso, Latin, and R&B tunes in addition to anything that was in a Panorama style. As NIU alumni Jeannine Remy recalled, his approach was very different, abandoning the more hackneyed tropical numbers.

> When Cliff came on the scene he changed all of this as he proclaimed, "Yellow Bird out the window man!" ... He quietly and patiently transformed us out of the nostalgic repertoire into a miniature Trini-style band. He could "real cuss us" when we did "stupidness" and in the next breath be the most loving person on the planet. A natural-born teacher, he had us learning tunes by rote that could make any West Indian look at us dumbfounded. The performance level of the group skyrocketed, and Al was beaming ear to ear knowing he had just hit the jackpot.[6]

As O'Connor would later note: "This guy has been playing pan for thirty years, what am I going to tell him about playing a calypso?"[7] By no means was O'Connor finished directing though, as he was still arranging new pieces for the band and directing the NIU Steelband through classical arrangements.

As co-leader of the band, Alexis had a less formal method of teaching, as former student James Walker remembered from the 1980s:

> Cliff was the less formal in my memory, but if you sat and asked him questions he could very clearly and articulately give you a sense of what he had in mind. A lot of times I'd be playing pan for someone else on a recital; they'd be playing the melody, and I'm strumming and I'm in the low range, and he would kind of lean over at rehearsal and say take this part up the octave, sounds muddy down there, I know you want the fullness of sound but it sounds muddy, take it up the octave. With his years of experience, of course, he knew exactly what to do, to fix that situation. He was more feedback than the classroom sort of study.[8]

Alexis and O'Connor had very different styles of arranging and rehearsing the NIU Steelband. O'Connor would often hand out fully notated charts and have the band work through parts. Other times he would hand out lead sheets with chord changes and common form structure indications (AABA, verse/chorus, etc). From the beginning, O'Connor did not rely on the traditions of rote learning so integral to steelbands in Trinidad. This did not change with the arrival of Alexis, as the latter realized immediately that he would need to adjust to the students at NIU and discern their background in sight reading.

Cliff Alexis had grown up in Trinidad with little formal music training, and most steelbands he performed in and those he later led and arranged music for all played by rote, with the various sections learned by watching others play the parts rather than working from scored-out parts. Since leaving Trinidad, Alexis had slowly made the change to notating his charts, and as a result the transition at NIU to working with music students who had grown up working with scored charts was not a difficult one. However, Alexis employed a mix of rote learning and note reading in his ensemble direction and challenged the students to focus on listening during the process. Alexis is fond of using the band as a large, ongoing experiment in arranging, and he was, and still is, notorious for handing out parts of an arrangement that he was working on, having the band learn and play them, then not being satisfied with the arrangement, have the parts passed in and changed. He was experimenting and pushing the boundaries of steelband arranging, and the NIU students got to witness the creative process firsthand.

Alexis's impact on the day-to-day rehearsal and artistic side of the NIU Steelband was immediate, and the program began creating a palpable buzz around campus at NIU. The students of NIU had to get used to Alexis, no doubt, and to the process of mixed rote learning and reading charts that he espoused during rehearsals. According to band member Lana Wordel, "You don't have to worry about reading notes, just about the music and how it feels."[9] Yet Alexis was undeterred by the students of NIU: "It's always a teaching process—university or no. The fact that they aren't Trinidadians playing what I want to play doesn't bother me. I can cultivate musicians here just like anywhere else."[10]

Ethnomusicologist Shannon Dudley of the University of Washington fondly remembered his time working at NIU and learning steelpan building from Alexis in 1985.

Dudley points out that despite his generosity, the steelband members at NIU were required to take matters seriously:

> For most of the students I met, steelband was just a chance to play cool music on a cool instrument. They didn't seem to have come there for a cultural experience, but they did have daily interaction with a panman who had been in steelband from near the start, and who wasn't going to take [guff] from any spoiled Midwestern music majors. Cliff often had to remind them where the instrument came from, and if they screwed around in rehearsal or disrespected the instrument or the music, he would share stories about people getting their heads busted for lesser offenses. I don't know if he ever busted any heads at NIU, but I know some students were afraid he might. They learned from him in a way they couldn't have learned in a class, or with a book. Despite Cliff's gruff manner and temper, he appreciated talent and commitment, and always had ambition to learn and move forward.[11]

Perhaps the most lasting impact of Alexis's addition to the NIU steelband faculty was his willingness and openness with his knowledge. Trinidadian panmen, notoriously protective of the steelpan, routinely accuse each other and foreigners of "stealing" steelpan and exploiting it for personal gain. The knowledge of how to build, tune, arrange, play, or teach steelpan is considered a trade secret, and the tight-lipped Trinidadians rarely give away such intellectual property. Alexis is different. He has made it a personal mission to bring steelpan to anyone interested in learning, even in the cornfields of Illinois. As a child in Trinidad, Alexis spent his days hanging out in the panyards from dawn to dusk. This act of liming (as it is known in Trinidad) results in one's being constantly surrounded by the steelpan and soaking up the knowledge. At NIU Alexis instituted by default, as a result of his personality, a similar tradition of liming around the NIU School of Music for steelpan majors. Alexis and O'Connor were both highly supportive of the informal education experience, and beyond the liming O'Connor and Alexis held countless informal classes on steelband history, technique, and arranging in various settings around the NIU campus. O'Connor and Alexis also began holding impromptu rehearsals to work on new and experimental steelband arrangements as students, according to Alexis, were "always hanging around just like in the panyard" and ready and eager to soak in the experience.[12] In this way, Alexis and O'Connor collectively brought the "panyard is a university" idea to NIU and instilled a tradition that was modeled by future NIU steelband hopefuls.

The fertile learning environment fostered by Alexis and O'Connor permeated the reaches of the School of Music, and many percussion majors with no intention of ever learning steelpan were sucked into the orbit of the NIU Steelband. This was the case for both Paul Ross and Elizabeth DeLamater. Ross recalled being transformed the moment he heard the steelband for the first time:

> I started at NIU in the fall in 1983, and in the spring of 1984 I played in a marimba band there, and we did an exchange concert with the University of Illinois. We went down to Urbana, and we were going to do a concert that night. The marimba band rehearsed, and then the steel

band rehearsed next. I really hadn't heard the band all year; a little bit in the distance but I hadn't signed up for it. I heard them rehearse and I almost ran up on stage; I mean I was so knocked out by the sound and even the tunes. So I was hooked from that point. I joined the next semester in the fall of '84.[13]

For DeLamater, her first exposure to the NIU steelband was accidental, but equally powerful:

> I went to NIU as a percussion major ... The third day of my college career in August of 1992 the steel band opened, and I was at the first rehearsal. I hadn't signed up but people were talking about it, drummers were talking about it, and the room opened up and somebody said are you coming? And all the amazing sound going on inside the room. And I said I don't know, should I? ... That was it. I fell in love right away. I couldn't believe how awesome it was by the end of the first rehearsal [and by] the end of the first week I was just so excited about it.[14]

Both DeLamater and Ross have since made a life in steelpan and teach the instrument as their primary occupation, all thanks to the environment fostered by Alexis and O'Connor. Their situations are not unique as dozens of NIU steelband alumni have gone on to plot a similar course in life.

FIGURE 4.2. Birch Creek steelband (mid-1980s)

The NIU–Birch Creek Connection

The successful synthesis of O'Connor and Alexis as a partnership in steelpan fostered the talents of many future pannists at NIU and throughout the Midwest. The impact of the NIU steelband program on the development of steelpan in the Midwest is nowhere more evident than their work at the Birch Creek Music Performance Center. Every summer beginning in 1982, O'Connor packed up a small assortment of steelpans and headed to Egg Harbor, Wisconsin to teach at the unconventional Birch Creek Music Performance Center summer music camp. Students at Birch Creek work very closely with music educators in a remote setting and perform for audiences comprised primarily of tourists (many from the Chicagoland area) vacationing in the scenic peninsula of Wisconsin's Door County. In one- or two-week sessions the camp features instruction on disciplines such as classical, jazz, and world music.

The tradition of summer music camps for aspiring high-school and college musicians has a long tradition in the United States, and famous programs such as the Interlochen Center for the Arts in Michigan, Brevard Music Center in Florida, and Tanglewood Music Center in Massachusetts are storied institutions with a history of classical-music excellence. The property on which the Birch Creek is located originally belonged to James Dutton, a Chicago native who was the percussion instructor at the American Conservatory of Music in Chicago. Dutton boasted a formidable stable of students, the most famous of which include Gordon Peters (percussionist with the Chicago Symphony and notable conductor) and Tom Siwe (who later became professor of percussion at the University of Illinois). Dutton and his wife Fran dreamed of turning their Door Country property into a performance venue, and this dream became reality in 1976 when they first opened the barn doors of Birch Creek to the public.

In order to set Birch Creek apart from the summer music-camp competitors, Dutton thought it would be exciting and unique to add world music to the program. Through various sources, Dutton was made aware of Cliff Alexis and his program in Minnesota, and contacted the panman with an offer to build a program. Alexis had heard negative things about Wisconsin from friends in Minnesota; weary of such offers, he declined the job and recommended O'Connor to establish the program even though, at the time, they had only recently met. O'Connor had also vacationed in the Door Country area with his family in the late 1970s and he agreed to try teaching steelpan at Birch Creek for one summer. One summer turned into thirty, and making the trip to Door County each summer became a regular part of O'Connor's summers, and occasionally Alexis's, from 1982–2012, when the steelband program was taken over by Liam Teague.

The camp is located in an isolated rural setting complete with farmhouse, barn, and silo. It is a place where "woodshedding" your music was to be taken literally; practice rooms were located in an old refurbished woodshed, and concerts are still to this day held in a converted barn.[15] The amenities were less than ideal though; several NIU/Birch Creek alumni, including Mike Schwebke, recall that this did little to dampen the spirits of the students and the quality of the experience:

It's funny, the steel band rehearses in arguably the worse part of the whole campus. There is an old, they call it a room, but it's where these cows used to be kept. It's a stone room in the back of the barn and it had two big barn doors on the back but it was about 125 degrees in there and no wind came through. There were fifteen pans packed into this tiny room.[16]

More recently, the Birch Creek Music Performance Center built a new rehearsal building where the steelband and other ensemble rehearsals are held. The upgrades to the facilities have done little to change the quaint surroundings.

The Birch Creek summer music academy was not simply a summer "gig" for O'Connor. From the beginning, the connection between Birch Creek and NIU was firmly established, and the Birch Creek summer music academy became, effectively, a summertime extension of college for NIU faculty, students, and staff. Following the addition of O'Connor, music faculty from NIU started joining the music teaching staff of the Birch Creek summer music academy, some intermittently (Rich Holly, Cliff Alexis, Jeff Stitely) and some permanently (Al O'Connor, Robert Chappell, and Liam Teague).

For NIU faculty, the Birch Creek summer music academy was an opportunity to teach, recruit new students for NIU, and socialize. For example, on his second trip to Birch Creek in 1991, percussionist Rich Holly had a life-changing experience: "I met my wife in 1991; it was the first Wednesday night of the camp, the faculty jazz concert. I was playing drum set, she was sitting in the front row, we smiled at each other frequently during the gig, I introduced myself afterwards, we went out for a drink, and the rest is history!"[17] The Birch Creek summer music academy also proved a fertile ground for recruiting graduate students for the NIU Steelband. For example, James Walker, who came to NIU in 1985 for the first of two graduate degrees, first became interested in steelpan and NIU when he attended Birch Creek as a percussionist. Walker was an undergraduate student at Ithaca College when he traveled to the summer camp, played with the steelband, and started talking to O'Connor about a future in music. According to Walker, "From his [O'Connor's] description between the pans and [world music], the strong jazz program at NIU, it was clear that their strengths at the school fit right with my interests."[18] Immediately following his Birch Creek experience, Walker bought a steelpan from Alexis and started playing on his own in anticipation of his start at NIU.

The success of the steelband program at the Birch Creek summer music academy was immediate, and Dutton sought to expand the world music offerings by hiring Robert Chappell in 1989. Two years later Chappell was appointed Birch Creek's director of percussion (a post he held until 2012), and thus an influx of students from NIU began coming to Birch Creek to assist the percussion session as teaching assistants or faculty. Over the years NIU teaching assistants have become a staple at Birch Creek and include Yuko Asada, Maggie Bergren, Doug Bratt, Frank Check, Adam Cowger, Elizabeth DeLamater, Kirk Hickman, Tom Hipskin, Denise Lowe, Aaron Puckett, Ben Runkel, Tim Rush, Suzanne Satterfield, Patrick Schleker, Chris Smith, Julie Stephens, John Tate, Ben Wahlund, and Erin Walker. Robert Chappell retired his post as director in 2012, and Ben Wahlund took over as the director of percussion at the Birch Creek summer music academy in 2013.

Although never mentioned in any formal programs, O'Connor often invited former students, such as co-author Jeannine Remy, back to Birch Creek to play alongside camp steelband students on steelpan or to fill in on keyboard parts if student deficits were not remedied during the weeklong camp.[19] Remy, herself a native of Door County, Wisconsin, began attending the Birch Creek summer music academy in 1978 while still a high school student. In addition to lending insight into the workings of Alexis and O'Connor as camp instructors, the following vignette illustrates her experience of attending the Birch Creek summer music academy and the transformative impact it had upon her career in music:

> I first met Al O'Connor during his second year at Birch Creek in 1983 when I was about to start my third year in college. Attending Lawrence Conservatory of Music at the time, I thought that it would be nice to learn some ethnic music, so I returned to Birch Creek. After that summer session in 1983, I fell in love with the steel drums and transferred to NIU. Al stated that the Birch Creek experience was like an unintentional recruiting ground for prospective high-school students and even those looking to continue on with their master's degrees. He told me, "I don't believe there were any other college students who transferred to NIU like you after coming to Birch Creek, but there were a number who decided to come as freshmen after attending and several who came as grad students after finishing their first degree."
>
> I remembered Al telling stories about how in 1982 he packed up his Suburban and headed for Door County ... a place he and his family had come to many times on vacation. Mr. Dutton arranged for Al to teach in the Shed the first couple of years. This meant that students had to cross County E [highway] and walk up a long gravel road near the A-frame, which at that time was Dutton's summer home that also doubled as the music faculty's residence. In the Shed was an entire family of steelpan instruments, a drum set and of course percussion (engine room/aux percussion). We were all percussionists so Al got right to work teaching us music on hand-scribbled sheets. Mr. Dutton wanted to show off the steelband right away so Al had to teach us enough music to play a gig at a local winery.
>
> The learning curve was intense, with no time to waste. We were placed behind an instrument and were told where to hit the notes, how to hit the notes, and then we began to learn the music by "finding" our notes. "Sink or swim," he said, so very quickly we had to learn how to strum, which notes of the chord to strum, and find any melodic lick we were asked to play. None of us knew the note patterns on the pan, but we quickly learned.
>
> The music repertoire was basically written as chord sheets and short melody "licks" whereby Al could play the melody on his "Bertie Marshall Style" double tenor and we would back him up. I remember pieces like "Anna," "Koka Yoka," "Bridge Over Troubled Water," "Evergreen," "[Hasely Crawford]," the "Disney Medley" (sometimes referred to as the "Kids Medley"), "Yellow Bird," "Island in the Sun," "Jamaica Farewell," and "Benwood Dick." In this little two-week session we had learned some old standard calypsos mixed with popular tunes that the crowd would recognize.
>
> This was my first introduction to the steelband and its music other than listening to old recordings with out-of-tune rustic sounding instruments. It was also my first introduction to Al's style of teaching, his infamous Al Speeches, and his passion for steelpans. I realized how

much fun it was, how one had to literally think on their feet, and how it was another avenue for creative expression in performance and arrangement. Although many perceived the instrument as a novelty, I gained a whole new appreciation for the art form as it clearly wasn't an instrument to be taken lightly. These memories came full circle in 2012 when I attended Al's last concert at Birch Creek. It was a tear-jerking moment for everyone except Al who held his stoic composure. Robert Chappell sat down at the piano and began playing one of the first songs Al taught us, "Bridge Over Troubled Water." Except for Al, there wasn't a dry eye in the audience.

Other students were greatly impacted by O'Connor's approach to teaching steelpan at Birch Creek. The brevity of the camp and the experience level of most students meant a steep learning curve. O'Connor, however, was a natural teacher, and his experience teaching pan at NIU for nearly a decade prior to the founding of the Birch Creek summer music academy was invaluable in teaching and communicating with the summer students. Another former Birch Creek summer music academy student and NIU alumni, Michael Bento, suggests that the program's strengths were the result of O'Connor's passionate involvement.

> Al started out the Wisconsin percussion/pan camp by explaining about the pans, basic technique, and so forth. He showed us the basic soca and calypso beats for the drum set (he could play them himself), and the percussion parts were taught and added. With regard to the pans, he taught us a simple bass line, the seconds and guitars strummed and maybe played a melodic line here and there, and the leads played the melody and we were off.
>
> Al always played with us and usually on double tenors, so pretty quickly we could hear the song coming together. He would allow some of us to improvise over the chord changes or he would, then return to the melody and end the song. Basically, he used a jazz format of head, solos, head. When the song was to end, Al would shout "out!" and that was the cue to take the song to the ending. Learning this from Al, I used this vocal "out" cue through all my future adult and student steel bands from then on.
>
> Al provided opportunities for all of us to play pans at the camp, allowing students to switch and try a new instrument for a new song. He gave the better players challenges to play harder and more complicated lines. I remember Al had an arrangement of the song "Africa" by Toto that he taught us. He had transcribed the entire keyboard solo, which he challenged another lead player and myself to learn note-for-note. We did learn that, played it in the culminating concert at the end of the camp, and felt great about our accomplishment. We felt pretty confident and proud of this little steel band in a short amount of time.[20]

Throughout the course of O'Connor's thirty years of teaching at the Birch Creek summer music academy, the musical repertoire slowly changed to meet the tastes and demographics of its audience. In addition to audience demographics, the presence of Alexis further influenced the repertoire choices at Birch Creek. Alexis, at the insistence of O'Connor, came to Birch Creek in the summer of 1984 and performed alongside the Birch Creek student steelband with a number of inner-city students from Minnesota. Members of Alexis's

Minnesota band included his son, Cliff Alexis, Jr., and a group of young men who would later become the nationally recognized pop group Mint Condition (Terry Fountain, Mark Haynes, Homer Odell, Dannie Young, and Stokley Williams). Despite the success of the concert, Alexis only visited Birch Creek twice in his career due to a few extenuating factors.[21] Despite his pleadings, O'Connor was only able to convince Alexis to come back to Door County and Birch Creek one more time, in 1988. Regardless, even to this day, Alexis has always supplied instruments for the summer camp at Birch Creek.

Alexis's physical absence at Birch Creek did not suppress his presence in spirit, and he greatly influenced the music repertoire that O'Connor selected to carry up to Door County. Because of Alexis's influence, O'Connor started teaching Birch Creek students more authentic Trinidadian-style music, some of it recently composed or arranged by Alexis. Although the O'Connor standards were still performed year after year as teaching tools for beginners, O'Connor gravitated toward Alexis's compositions along with transcriptions of Len "Boogsie" Sharpe's works. Moving beyond the single-page chord change charts favored by O'Connor, the Alexis-inspired compositions had more notes and less strumming. This includes pieces such as "Confusion Reggae," "Rock Yuh Pan Man," "Try Jah Love," "Power," "Sunset," "Song to Chiricahau," "Summer Song," and "Pan Rising," which, although not Panorama tunes, were significant elevations in difficulty.

Whereas Alexis chose to stay away from Birch Creek, Liam Teague's experience was much different, and Door Country/Birch Creek welcomed him with open arms, first as a soloist and eventually as teacher and O'Connor's replacement. Teague first came to Birch Creek in 1995 and stunned the Door County audiences with his quick hands, creative improvisations, and prodigious talent. During his first season at Birch Creek, Teague was billed as a "special performer," and he was only twenty-one years old. After the 1995 season, Teague became a faculty member at Birch Creek, and like Alexis, his arrangements and compositions have appeared on the concert programs ever since. Upon O'Connor's retirement from Birch Creek in the summer of 2012, Liam Teague assumed the directorship of the steelband program there and is assisted by Yuko Asada.

The students who attended the percussion sessions of the Birch Creek summer music academy are mostly high-school age (though plenty of college students from NIU and elsewhere have attended), and the majority are from the Chicago metro and Wisconsin areas. Many of these young Birch Creek percussionists study privately with teachers associated with NIU, making the recruiting ties to the steelband and percussion program at NIU ever stronger.

From its small and humble beginnings in 1982, the reputation and size of the steelband program at the Birch Creek summer music academy grew, and each year the performance level of the students increased as students were competitively auditioning to participate in the camp. More buildings, practice rooms, dormitories, and facilities were added, and teams of fundraisers were able to secure large financial donations from the Door County community.

Over the years a wealth of scholarships assisted talented steelpan participants who did not otherwise have the funds to attend the Birch Creek summer music academy. For several years the Washington D.C. based CAFÉ program(Cultural Academy for Excellence) sent two steelpan students to Birch Creek when scholarships were available.[22] For more than two decades, the CAFÉ has been one of the leading programs in the United States promoting the steelpan as an educational and empowerment tool. Many of the students from the CAFÉ program are from low-income backgrounds and the Birch Creek experience is an invaluable opportunity and support mechanism for talented youth. In 2012, the music program at the University of the West Indies (UWI) was asked to conduct auditions for scholarships for Trinidadian students to attend Birch Creek. The auditions were conducted in April of 2013, and two qualified participants were selected to study abroad at the camp. The Pat Bishop Scholarship Fund set up by Trinidadian steelpan patron Mark Loquan and the Music Literacy Trust of Trinidad and Tobago (of which Liam Teague was a founding member) funded the travel and tuition to Birch Creek for the Trinidadian students, and further cemented the bond between NIU and UWI as further discussed in Chapter 10.[23]

CHAPTER 5

GUEST ARTISTS THROUGHOUT THE YEARS

> I just want you all to know that I consider this concert today with the NIU steelband a real breakthrough in my career. And I want to thank Liam, Cliff, and NIU for this opportunity!
> —Freddy Harris III (2012)[1]

For any college or university performing ensemble, featuring a guest artist or soloist is a steadfast way to challenge student performers, elevate the overall quality of the ensemble, and invigorate the student body of the institution. In addition to such benefits, guest artists often bring new or different cultural perspectives to a region unaccustomed to meeting individuals from a specific part of the world. Guest artists represent a chance for faculty members to bring in outside experts with the hope that they, too, can learn from the experience and skill of the specialist. Finally, guest artists allow music ensembles, and even entire music programs, the opportunity for marketing and publicity that hopefully will reach a wider audience beyond the campus, drawing in the public and perspective students to the campus. The inherent benefits of visiting guest artists aside, such luxuries are expensive, and funding these outside experts is a challenge for most music departments and schools of music throughout the United States. This fact alone makes the appearance of such an artist a rare occasion on most university campuses across the United States.

Since the inception of the percussion program at NIU in 1968, O'Connor had felt very strongly that bringing guest artists to campus was an integral part of the NIU experience. The vast array of world music instruments and musical traditions that fall within the auspices of percussion, too vast for one individual to master, present challenges for percussion students and professors at colleges and universities across the United States. For the past fifty years the expectation that college-level percussion students can master an ever-expanding number of instruments that individually require a lifetime of study in order to develop mastery has steadily increased, and many percussionists choose to specialize as they advance along the path of their degree studies. For this very reason, O'Connor insisted on bringing leading national and international figures in percussion performance to the NIU campus as guests throughout his teaching and administrative career. This included guest timpanists, multi-percussionists (Nexus), drum set players (Louis Bellson), xylophonists (Bob Becker), marimbists (Leigh Howard Stevens, Keiko Abe, Gordon Stout), vibraphonists (Brad Stirtz, David Samuels), and of course, a cavalcade of steelpan players and builders.

The guest artists who worked specifically with the NIU Steelband reflect the development of the band over the course of its history. That is to say that as the NIU Steelband progressed from sharing concerts with the percussion ensemble, Musica Exotica series, and Rosewood-n-Steel concerts shared with the NIU marimba ensemble in the 1970s into the early 1980s, to the Alexis era starting in 1985, the guests artists also changed to reflect the developments of steelpan in Trinidad and the United States. Regardless of the sea change, one thing that remained constant from year to year was the consistently high quality of the steelpan guest artists. O'Connor and Alexis made a practice of seeking out the best and brightest stars of the steelpan world to perform with the NIU Steelband and to inspire the NIU student body. Even to this day, soloing with the NIU Steelband serves as a benchmark for up-and-coming steelpan soloists the world over, as evidenced by the performances of young virtuosos Freddy Harris III and Jonathan Scales.

The strong tradition of the NIU Steelband hosting guest artists was a tradition forged by O'Connor and Alexis collectively. In fact, prior to the arrival of Alexis in 1985 as a member of the NIU music faculty, the NIU Steelband featured very few guest soloists during its first decade. This was due to several factors, the two most pressing of which were access to quality steelpan soloists and the NIU Steelband concert structure. The NIU Steelband began performing in 1973; however, its first official concert performance was with the NIU percussion ensemble in 1974. From 1975 to 1981, the NIU Steelband shared concerts with the NIU percussion ensemble and also performed as part of the Musica Exotica series started by ethnomusicology professor Dr. Han, which featured all the world music ensembles at NIU in annual concerts known for their diverse offerings and exhausting length. In 1981 the NIU Steelband broke from the NIU percussion ensemble and the Musica Exotica series and, along with the NIU marimba ensemble, performed annually in the spring as part of a concert series aptly titled Rosewood-n-Steel. It was after the establishment of the Rosewood-n-Steel concert format (in which each ensemble presented half the concert) that the NIU Steelband started to invite guest soloists on a more regular basis.

In the spring of 1990, the NIU Steelband changed its concert format, ceased performing with the NIU marimba band, and set out to forge a new tradition of hosting annual concerts of steelband only in the spring of each academic year. O'Connor was worried that the concerts were becoming too long. He told the campus paper *Northern Today* that a change was necessary. "The groups have now reached a maturity level that requires a separate program—otherwise we would have the audience in there for most of the afternoon."[2] From 1991 to the present, the NIU Steelband has performed stand-alone concerts every spring. With the growing strength of the program came added requests for performances. To satisfy these requests, the NIU Steelband added a fall concert to the schedule in 2007 and has since performed stand-alone concerts every fall and spring—almost all featured a different guest artist.

The arrival of Alexis in 1985 changed the outlook of the NIU Steelband toward guest artists both artistically and financially. First, with Alexis on staff as a builder/tuner/co-director of the NIU steelband, O'Connor could now use the funds generated by the band's many gigs and engagements for the purpose of hiring guest artists rather than buying steelpans, hiring steelpan tuners, and paying for instrument upkeep. With Alexis on staff, this previously earmarked money became liquid, and O'Connor put it to good use by, among other things, bringing in guest artists. O'Connor created what is known to this day as the "local fund" from which guest artists were paid.[3] Cash from NIU Steelband gigs came in, and cash to guest artists went out.

The simple cash flow system allowed him to bypass the clumsy accounting measures of the university allocation system as well as pay, in a timely manner, guest artists from the Caribbean. The fund required no allocation or line item from the state of Illinois, and O'Connor simply had to note the fund balance at the beginning and end of each fiscal year. Other NIU ensembles that performed gigs and hosted international guest artists, such as the NIU Jazz Band, had similar funds set for such occasions, and the simplicity and hands-off nature of the "local fund" allowed the NIU steelband program to operate in a pseudo-independent fashion from the NIU School of Music. Another benefit of the "local fund" was O'Connor's ability to ask for the funds in cash. If, say, David Rudder was coming to NIU to perform with the band, O'Connor would request the funds several days ahead of time, have the Trinidadian sign an honorarium form upon arrival, and hand the guest artist cash on the spot. "I remember when David Rudder came to perform with us. I met him at that hotel and said 'Is your room ok? Good,' and then I handed him ... cash in an envelope."[4]

The second change with Alexis as a permanent faculty member was the type of guest soloists the NIU Steelband invited to perform with the band. Prior to Alexis's joining the faculty at NIU, O'Connor invited mostly American or American-based steelbands and steelpan soloists to perform as guest artists. These included elite American steelbands—of which there were a select few—such as the US Navy Steel Band in 1982 and the University of Illinois Steelband (which O'Connor helped establish) in 1984—and the internationally known steelpan soloist Andy Narell, who came to NIU several times from 1982 to 1985.[5] Andy Narell, perhaps the best-known pannist in the world and a world-class soloist, no doubt energized the NIU Steelband; however, Alexis saw a different dimension to the idea of guest soloists. As O'Connor recalls, "Alexis was kind of in a Trinidad mode at that point. Meaning that he wanted us to stop asking Andy to come and bring people like Boogsie."[6] For Alexis, the situation was neither an indictment of Narell nor his skill set; rather, it was a

FIGURE 5.1. NIU Steelband with Andy Narell (1985)

broader look at the many talented panmen in Trinidad who, lacking resources, never leave the island.

The history of steelpan in Trinidad is often one of lost opportunity, and Alexis took it upon himself to see that pannists from Trinidad had the opportunity to be seen and heard in the United States. Alexis was interested in spreading steelpan around the world and in elevating the respect and perceptions of the program at NIU. O'Connor had sold Alexis on the mission/vision of the NIU steelband program; now it was up to Alexis to sell the very same mission/vision to a skeptical, and often dismissive, Trinidadian faction of pannists who were proud of the Trinidadian tradition and concerned about American encroachment into the realm of their national instrument.

With the exception of Alexis, the first Trinidadian guest artist to come to DeKalb was Len "Boogsie" Sharpe, who came in the spring of 1988. Boogsie was a guest soloist with the NIU Steelband for the triumphant PASIC mass band performances in St. Louis during the fall of 1987, and Alexis and O'Connor were eager to get Sharpe on campus to share his expertise in a more intimate setting. Sharpe was a close personal friend of Alexis since his youth back in Trinidad, and booking him as a guest artist at NIU was a relatively simple arrangement.

Other guest artists to perform at NIU in the late 1980s were Trinidadians already in the United States for reasons beyond steelpan. These included Leonard Moses, a former member of the Desperados Steel Orchestra, who had lived in the United States since 1975. Herald Headley was another Trinidadian living in the United States who performed as a guest artist with the NIU Steelband in 1987. Headley met Alexis in 1967 when the two performed (in separate bands—Alexis with the National Steel Orchestra of Trinidad and Tobago and Headley with the Tripoli Steelband) in Montreal for Expo 67.[7] Once Alexis discovered that Headley was in the United States attending a local college some 150 miles from DeKalb (University of Wisconsin–Oshkosh), the invitation was sent. As Headley recalls, "I don't know how he [Alexis] knew I was there, but he found out I was in Wisconsin and called me, and we set it up that I would come and play at NIU as a guest artist."[8]

Moses and Headley were so impressed with the program at NIU that they eventually became graduate students there, and both earned master of music degrees in percussion (Moses in 1983 and Headley in 1991) with a focus in steelpan. However, these pannists were already established in the United States. Coaxing the best and brightest of the Trinidadian steelpan world to come to DeKalb directly from Trinidad proved challenging throughout the late 1980s, and only a select few stalwarts—Sharpe, for example—made the trip north to perform. Alexis believed strongly in the importance of having Trinidadian guest artists every year; however, the expectations of the Trinidadians and the lack of respect (or ignorance) they had for non-Trinidadian steelband programs was blatantly obvious. "Sometimes he [Alexis] would call and they [Trinidadian pannists] would be a little standoffish,

FIGURE 5.2. NIU Steelband with Leonard Moses

and they would ask for an enormous amount of money. We would have to say we pay our guest artists this much, we pay your plane ticket up here, we pay your hotel."[9]

The perceptions of the NIU Steelband changed greatly following the rousing success of the first Taiwan tour in 1992. The tour received a great deal of press coverage from local, regional, and national newspapers in the United States, newspapers in Asia, *The Chronicle of Higher Education*, and several newspapers in Trinidad and Tobago. With this increased attention came increased prestige for the NIU steelband program, and nowhere was this more evident than in Trinidad and Tobago. The NIU Steelband beat globetrotting Trinidadian steelbands to the prize of becoming the first steelband of any kind to tour Taiwan. Further, perhaps the most lasting impact resulting from the press blitz generated in Trinidadian newspapers from the NIU Steelband's 1992 Taiwan tour was that many Trinidadian panmen, now convinced of the NIU Steelband's legitimacy, started to respect the NIU steelband program. It also became easier for the band to book guest artists from Trinidad, the greater Caribbean, the United States, and even to book the celebrated jazz pannist Rudy "Two Left" Smith, who traveled all the way from Copenhagen to play with the NIU steelband.

According to O'Connor, the about-face was rather telling. "They were now calling us, offering to come up and play for our fee that we told them they could have."[10] The added attention on a regional level around DeKalb and Chicago, too, was a boon to the NIU steelband program as requests for local performances by the NIU Steelband at primary and secondary schools and the like increased threefold. The added performances meant added dollars to the "local fund," which in turn led to increased funds to spend on guest artists. From this point onward to the present day, with few exceptions (such as the concert following the return from the Taiwan 1998 spring concert), the NIU Steelband has featured a different guest artist in addition to faculty from the NIU School of Music for almost every one of their concerts.

TABLE 5.1. NIU STEELBAND GUEST ARTISTS

Artist	Year
US Navy Steel Band	1982
Lennard Moses	1983
University of Illinois Steelband, Thomas Siwe, and Cliff Alexis	1984
Cliff Alexis	1984
Andy Narell	1985
Brad Stirtz	1986
Leonard Moses and Neville York	1987
Harold Headley	1987
Len "Boogsie" Sharpe	1988, 1990, 1996, 1997
Rudy Smith	1989
Robert Greenidge	1991, 1993, 2013
Ray Holman	1994

Guest Artists Throughout the Years

David Rudder	2003
Orlando Cotto and Dave Hartsman	2004
Ai Ishida	2005
Victor Provost	2010
Chris Tanner and the University of Miami Steelband	2010
Leon "Foster" Thomas	2011
Freddy Harris III	2012
Jonathan Scales	2012
Jeannine Remy	2012
Andre White	2013
Graciela "Chelín" Núñez	2014
Etienne Charles	2014
NIU Wind Ensemble	2015
NIU Jazz Orchestra	2016

CHAPTER 6

ON THE ROAD—THE NIU STEELBAND TOURS AMERICA

An important component of any university music program is performance. In some programs that may be limited to a few campus events, but O'Connor was committed to giving the students in the NIU Steelband as broad a performance experience as possible. Opportunities ranged from local concerts around DeKalb to as far away as he could arrange. Early in the band's history the range of performances included tours to the East Coast during the late spring and summer built around O'Connor's home base in Long Island. In addition, the NIU Steelband embarked on several major trips outside the Chicagoland area over the course of its history. The NIU Steelband also trekked forth on several notable tours to professional conferences and meetings such as several trips to PASIC (Percussive Arts Society International Convention) and the 1995 Acoustical Society of America national meeting in St. Louis. Beyond the publicity and prestige generated by the NIU Steelband on these various tours, O'Connor and Alexis sought a hands-on educational experience for NIU Steelband members, and these tours served as a laboratory for experiencing life on the road as a professional musician.

"Run Out" Concerts

The most common off-campus events were a regular series of daytime school programs known as "run out" concerts. O'Connor saw these as an important part of the NIU Steelband's mission. These concerts consisted of performances of eight to ten standard songs or tunes with no extended or overly difficult repertoire performed for local or regional school-age children. Steadfast in his desire to educate the masses about the history and culture of steelband music, O'Connor (and later Alexis and Teague) insisted that the format of these school concerts include plenty of room for presenting the full picture of steelband, history and all.

> You can't talk about Al and his performances without mentioning his notorious "Al Speeches." It was a sort of a "stall tactic" as there wasn't always a gig list, as he would feel out the audiences as we played, and he would simply "call out the tune" and expect us to find it in our folder and "clothes pin it up" while he "educated" the audience. These speeches were bits and pieces of steelband history that informed the audience more on the culture and music of Trinidad and Tobago.[1]

O'Connor viewed these concerts as a dual educational opportunity—that is, educational for the audience to learn about steelband and educational for the NIU Steelband students to learn how to present and perform public concerts of this professional sort and style. The typical concert format consisted of the band playing a few tunes, a discussion of steelband and Trinidadian history, an instrument demo of each of the steelband voices, concluding with several more tunes.

According to co-author Jeannine Remy, "Al was the kind of person who liked the music to fit on one page." This affinity for concise sheet music was created, perhaps out of necessity, because, during this time, NIU's means of copying was a mimeographing machine. The sheet music was handwritten (in O'Connor's eclectic left-handed screed) and mostly as chord charts with occasional "licks" that were scored briefly or just plain letter names in the direction of the music. Students had to be able to read a musical road map and know and understand chords, chord voicings, and corresponding rhythmic patterns, the aptly named "Al strum."[2]

The NIU Steelband had the set list down to a science and rotated a mix of about twenty tunes. The repertoire itself consisted of calypso, pop tunes, classical tunes, jazz tunes—essentially the full spectrum available to steelbands at the time. O'Connor led the band from behind his "Bertie Marshall style" double tenor steelpan cuing and signaling the band as Remy recalled.

> While playing with one hand and raising the other with a simple turn around "Out!" shout that meant the solo was done and we were moving back to the head. He never missed a beat, and to this day I can envision him stomping his foot, conducting and playing. I might also add that before Cliff, Al was the soloist improvising over the chord changes, and he was really good, especially on the piece called 'The.'[3]

Every late spring during the early years of the NIU Steelband—approximately 1975–1978—O'Connor assembled a small steelband comprised of NIU students and toured the East Coast. O'Connor took advantage of the overlap between the public-school academic year and the NIU academic year. The typical grade school year runs approximately one month longer than the NIU school year, and upon the completion of the spring semester, O'Connor would gather a group of ten to twelve interested steelband students, rehearse, load the vans, and head east. A major impetus for the tours was financial—earning money for the NIU steelband program to buy more steelpans and tune the existing instruments. In order to make the tours viable and profitable, O'Connor restricted the size of the band so that the entire entourage, steelpans and people, fit into two large university-owned passenger vans.

O'Connor used the connections he had from growing up on Long Island as a means to book concerts at grade schools and community organizations throughout the region. Between O'Connor's alma mater school district in central Long Island and the former colleagues of O'Connor and his wife Judith (a choir director and voice teacher), the NIU Steelband soon had plenty of requests for concerts, and in more than one instance, had to decline extra requests for performances due to a fully booked schedule. Further, Judith's father was an elementary-school principal on Long Island, and he too aided in securing performances for the NIU Steelband. The East Coast tours lasted from ten days to three weeks, and O'Connor and the NIU students stayed with O'Connor's extended family and friends as well as members of the Islip Yacht Club in an effort to keep the tours profitable. The "run out" concerts of the East Coast tours were grueling, and the band would play thirty to forty concerts in the span of two weeks.

During the East Coast tour in 1976, O'Connor was presented with an opportunity to record an album with the NIU Steelband. Through networking and word of mouth, O'Connor was introduced to a recording engineer in Long Island who had open space in his recording studio on one of the days that O'Connor and the steelband would be in the area. Seizing the opportunity, O'Connor and the band spent an entire day at a recording studio in Huntington Station, New York, recording an album titled *The N.I.U. Steel Band Plays Calypso-Pop-Classics*. The album was released on the Silver Crest Custom label and was the first album release for the NIU Steelband. Silver Crest Custom had a reputation for recording projects such as the NIU Steelband, and the label regularly recorded local secondary-school and college ensembles for vanity pressings during the 1970s.[4] O'Connor ordered an initial pressing of 500 albums and sold them at concerts, gigs, and at PASIC 1977 as a means of generating funds for the NIU steelband program. The repertoire for the album reflects that of the "run out" concerts and includes several calypso arrangements such as "The Happy Wanderer," "Yellow Bird," "Matilda," "A Trinidad Song," and "Amelia Rose." The album also included an eclectic mix of arrangements such as "Kids Medley" (Disney tunes), "Beatles Medley," "Disco Medley," selections from *Jesus Christ Superstar*, and the "Air" from the English Suite No. 3 for Harpsichord by J. S. Bach.

The East Coast concerts were important on many levels for the NIU students and the NIU steelband program. First, O'Connor saw these tours as a real-world educational experience. Many of the NIU students were destined for careers as professional musicians on their primary instruments, and negotiating life while traveling on the road for weeks at a time with band mates (not necessarily friends) is an important skill only duplicated in a scenario such as these tours. Second, these East Coast tours were a major source of revenue

FIGURE 6.1. NIU Steelband Album Cover Photo (1976)

for the NIU steelband program. O'Connor saw them as an integral part of insuring enough funding to maintain the existing steelpans and to purchase new instruments as the ensemble grew in size.

For the students who took part in these East Coast tours, the experience was priceless. O'Connor was sensitive to the students' well-being and gave the option of doing more or fewer concerts each day on tour. As James Campbell notes, "If we did extra, we could use that to pay for a seafood dinner. Most of us Midwesterners had only experienced seafood in the form of fried catfish or fish sticks on Friday nights at home, so this was also an opportunity for us to experience new culinary styles. We ate steamed clams, lobsters, and corn."[5] The good times were not to last, however. By 1978 O'Connor was finding it difficult to find housing for the NIU students on the tours, and the burden of organizing the tours outweighed the benefits. The East Coast tours were a product of their time, and O'Connor commented, "These tours would never work nowadays. Gas is too expensive, and grade schools have no money for music."[6]

PASIC

In addition to the countless tours throughout the Midwest and the East Coast, the NIU Steelband has thus far made repeated appearances at the Percussive Arts Society International

Convention (PASIC). The band first went in 1977 (Knoxville, Tennessee) and again in 1981 as part of a dedicated focus on world music (Indianapolis), and in 1987 (St. Louis), and 1994 (Atlanta) with the full large-size NIU Steelband. The Percussive Arts Society was founded in 1961 and is the premier academic and professional organization for all things percussion in the United States as well as many parts of the globe. With twenty-eight chapters around the world, the Percussive Arts Society is an international organization that boasts a membership in excess of 7,000 members.

The annual international convention (PASIC) began in 1976 and regularly draws in excess of 6,000 attendees. From its humble beginnings PASIC has grown into a showcase for leading international performers, academics, and instrument developers from the world of percussion.[7] A well-received performance at PASIC can make or break the career of an up-and-coming percussionist striving for national or international exposure, and most college percussion programs consider an invitation to perform at PASIC a program benchmark.

The lecture and performance of O'Connor and a small band of pannists from the NIU Steelband at PASIC 1977 was notable for many reasons. It was, by all accounts, the first time that steelband had been featured at PASIC. The convention was a much smaller affair in 1977 than now (only two days instead of four, with an attendance in the hundreds instead of the thousands), though the inclusion of steelpan was no less significant. O'Connor was scheduled to go on in the early afternoon on the convention's first day, a prime spot in the schedule. According to the PASIC 1977 official program, the lecture and demonstration was billed as a clinic, and the NIU Steelband as "the only actively playing steel band in an American University. The music spans a wide range from contemporary American popular music to authentic Caribbean selections and transcriptions of popular classics. Especially effective is the group's historical presentation of the origins of steel band music."[8] The clinic and performance was a success, and several individuals attribute seeing NIU at this PASIC as their inspiration for starting steelbands at their own respective institutions.[9] Interestingly, not all who attended were supportive of O'Connor and his endeavors at NIU. After the clinic, two influential professors of percussion from reputable universities approached O'Connor and offered congratulations for the performance. However, the pair then proceeded to disparage steelband music and O'Connor's efforts, telling him, "You shouldn't be messing with this [steelband]. It's never going anyplace."[10] Luckily, O'Connor did not heed their advice.

With the successful reception of steelpan at PASIC 1977, O'Connor forged ahead with the steelband program at NIU. In 1981 the NIU Steelband returned to the convention and made its first appearance at PASIC as a full band. O'Connor and company were invited to perform as one of the showcase concerts at the event, which was being held just a short drive down the road in Indianapolis. The performance came on the heels of the publication of the Spring/Summer 1981 *Percussive Notes* journal—guest edited by O'Connor—which was dedicated exclusively to steelband. With the PASIC 1981 performance, the NIU Steelband displayed the best possible face of steelband to the greater membership of the Percussive Arts Society and won over many skeptical percussionists. In particular, O'Connor was excited about the reception of an arrangement of "Mas in May," which by all accounts was the first Trinidadian Panorama–style arrangement performed at PASIC by any steelband. "People had never heard a Panorama tune live and when we played that Sparrow tune, 'Mas in May,' to close the show it really blew them away."[11]

The band was undoubtedly well received in Indianapolis for PASIC 1981; however, despite that success it would be another decade before the NIU Steelband would make a lasting impact at PASIC. By late 1986, Alexis was firmly established as a part of NIU and O'Connor was eager to show off the drastic improvement of the band and again take them to PASIC. Rather than a solo concert featuring the NIU Steelband, O'Connor and Alexis proposed hosting a mass steelband: featuring steelbands from across the United States together with the NIU Steelband as the central lynchpin. O'Connor was interested in making a band the size of a panorama band in Trinidad (100 or so players), and he thought it would be fun to see if they could do it.[12] PASIC 1987 was held in St. Louis, and O'Connor argued that the central location of the city within the greater United States would draw steelbands from a variety of universities, especially the Midwest. The organizing committee agreed, and the mass steelband was scheduled for PASIC 1987.

Len "Boogsie" Sharpe was already scheduled to appear at PASIC 1987 to give a steelpan clinic, and O'Connor and Alexis arranged for Sharpe to join their proposed mass band as a featured soloist. Alexis composed the arrangements for the mass band and used two tunes, the Panorama masterpiece "Pan in A Minor" and calypsonian David Rudder's "The Hammer," to perform with the other mass band steelbands. Unlike PASIC 1977, the performance time slot for PASIC 1987 was abysmal—10 a.m. As O'Connor recalls, "The only rehearsal we had was at two in the morning, the morning of the concert. So it was like go in there and keep your fingers crossed."[13] Former NIU steelpan student Lenard Moses played drum set, and the performance went swimmingly without incident or collapse.

Along with the NIU steelband the following steelbands performed in the mass steelband titled "Panorama—U.S.A.": the University of Akron Steel Band, the American Conservatory of Music Steel Express, the Brigham Young University Steel Band, the Harper College Steel Band, the University of Illinois Steel Band, the Indiana State University Steel Band, the James Madison University Steel Band, the North Texas State University Steel Band, the St. Bernard-Elmwood Place High School Steel Band, the University of South Dakota Steel Drum Band, Stainless Steel, A Tropical Steel Band Trio, the Waubonsee College Steel Band (Illinois), the West Liberty State College Steel Band, and the Western Illinois University Steel Band. Some sent three or four players, and others sent ten or more. The total number of players was approximately 110 individual pannists, and the mass band exceeded the expectations of O'Connor and Alexis. To bring together in the United States so many pannists to perform two arrangements was a huge accomplishment and a major feat of organizational perseverance. The performance was a rousing success, and PAS organizers considered it one of the highlights of PASIC that year.

Following the NIU Steelband's highly successful tour of Taiwan in 1992, O'Connor was interested in keeping the momentum moving forward. With the success of the Taiwan tour in hand, the prestige of the NIU Steelband had never been higher, and O'Connor and

Alexis were hopeful that PASIC 1994 would again provide an opportunity for the band to perform. Despite his optimism, O'Connor had heard through various sources that the PASIC program committee was not about to host the NIU Steelband so soon following the 1987 mass band. Changing strategies, he proposed a joint concert with the West Virginia University Steelband in which Ellie Mannette and Alexis would be honored for their contributions to the development of steelband in Trinidad and Tobago and the United States. The PASIC scheduling panel accepted their proposal, and arrangements were set in motion. For PASIC 1994, the NIU Steelband and the West Virginia University Steelband would share the stage, with each band performing separate pieces as well as two combined numbers. Alexis and O'Connor offered the NIU signature piece "Wood-n-Steel" by Robert Chappell as one of the combined steelband pieces; the other was Ray Holman's "Panic," which was transcribed by NIU Steelband members for the occasion. Like Len "Boogsie" Sharpe in 1987, Ray Holman was brought in from Trinidad to be a guest soloist with the joint steelbands in an effort to lend further excitement and prestige to the concert.

The NIU Steelband further used PASIC 1994 as a platform to show off two of its prized members—Alexis and Teague. The two were featured in a joint lecture panel titled "The State of the Art of Pan in Trinidad and Elsewhere" as part of the PASIC focus day program. Later that same evening, Teague (with Alexis as a guest accompanist) was a soloist in a feature concert that celebrated young talent in world music. This was Teague's second year at NIU, and though he was a well-known commodity in Trinidad and Tobago, the PASIC concert announced his prodigious talents to the greater percussion world. Teague dazzled the audience with his skills and further earned their adoration through the quality of his original compositions, "A Visit to Hell" and "Etude for Cello."

With PASIC 1994 buzzing from Teague's performance, the conference then shifted to the joint steelband concert two days later. The concert was given the rather lengthy title "A Concert in Honor of the Accomplishments of Cliff Alexis and Ellie Mannette toward the Advancement of Steelpan in the United States." The NIU Steelband and the West Virginia University Steelband each performed works separately and combined for the mass selections. Alexis and Mannette were presented with plaques of appreciation from the Percussive Arts Society by Larry Snider of the University of Akron, an accomplished pannist and steelband director in his own right. In all, the concert was well attended, and the feedback was very positive. Several attendees commented that this was a fine showing by the two finest university steelbands in the United States.[14]

For the NIU Steelband, the trip to and from Atlanta was not a direct route. In fact, O'Connor was never one to miss a performance opportunity, and the NIU Steelband played several concerts both on the way to and returning from Atlanta, creating a short tour. On the way to Atlanta, the band played concerts in Akron, Ohio at the University of Akron and at the Woodward Academy in Atlanta. On the way back to DeKalb from Atlanta, the band played a joint concert with the University of Kentucky Steelband in Lexington, Kentucky, hosted by NIU alumnus James Campbell.

In recent years the NIU Steelband faculty has continued a very active schedule of performances and clinics at PASIC. These include PASIC 2011, in which Teague shared the stage with marimbist Kevin Bobo (Indiana University) and was a featured member of Dr. Chris Hanning's (West Chester University) mass steelband. At PASIC 2015 Teague once again shared the stage with former NIU percussion professor Robert Chappell as part of a world music presentation.

The Acoustical Society of America

Following the successful tour to Atlanta for PASIC 1994, the NIU Steelband returned to DeKalb with a mind to look for different domestic venues in which to perform. With the increased visibility from their recent tours to Taiwan and elsewhere, the band was a highly sought-after commodity regionally, and there was no shortage of performance requests in and around DeKalb and the Chicagoland area. With no major cross-country or international tours on the horizon, O'Connor and Alexis used the opportunity to pursue a project with NIU physics professor Thomas D. Rossing.

For years, the NIU Steelband and Alexis's office on the second floor of the School of Music building had served as an extended laboratory for Rossing, who was fascinated with the sound of the steelpan. Rossing and O'Connor had been colleagues for many years (Rossing began working at NIU in 1971), and as O'Connor built the NIU Steelband, Rossing fostered a well-respected body of research in the science and acoustics of musical instruments. One of his areas of specialty was his interest in the sounds of pan. By 1995, Rossing had presented numerous conference papers on the acoustics of steelpan and published many of these in scholarly journals.[15] His work with the NIU Steelband would later comprise a significant portion of his book-length publication, *The Science of Percussion Instruments* (2001).[16]

Rossing was particularly interested in the science of the steelpan and was drawn to Alexis. Attempting to explain the process and scientific principles of the steelpan is something that has perplexed scientists in Trinidad and America for decades. In the late 1950s, Admiral Daniel Gallery of the US Navy Steel Band was determined to unlock the scientific secrets of the steelpan, though to no avail. As early as 1957, Admiral Gallery commented to folk singer Pete Seeger that:

> "My metallurgists tell me that heating the drum over a bonfire is a lot of hokum. They claim the temperature doesn't get hot enough to effect the physical properties of the steel. However, I tell them that since you and [Ellie] Mannette insist that it's necessary, maybe it affects the spiritual qualities that don't show up on Brinell hardness testers, or on strain gages, or chemical analysis."[17]

Indeed, one need only spend a short time with Alexis or O'Connor to hear one of the countless stories of perplexed audience members upon hearing the steelpan for the first time. Rossing, however, was determined to shed light on the mystery of the steelpan's sound, and in Alexis he had an experienced craftsman in residence at NIU whom he could ply with nuanced questions regarding the principles of design, construction, and acoustics. Why do steelpan builders fire heat the steelpans? Why are the skirts different lengths for each steelpan? As Alexis recalls, "This guy, he comes in here and he asks a question, takes a measurement, asks another question and so on, this went on for months!"[18] Having an experienced steelpan builder on hand allowed Rossing the ability to conduct meaningful research on steelpans throughout the entire process of their creation. This included measuring steel strength and elasticity before and after firing.[19] Alexis became, in a sense, a research partner of Rossing and was a cited co-author on several of the physicist's scholarly papers.

With his growing body of research on the steelpan reaching a critical mass, Rossing began presenting several research papers at the annual conferences of the Acoustical Society of America (ASA) throughout the 1980s and 1990s. With the annual ASA conference scheduled to take place in St. Louis in December of 1995, Rossing, Alexis, and O'Connor saw an opportunity for the NIU Steelband. Roughly 300 miles from DeKalb, St. Louis was a reasonable distance for the NIU Steelband to travel, and Rossing applied to the ASA for an entire panel on the steelpan at the conference. The panel was comprised of the papers "The Acoustics of Steelpan" by Rossing, Uwe Hanson, and David Hanson; "Construction and Tuning of Steelpan" by Alexis; "The History and Development of the Steelpan" by O'Connor; and "The Music of the Steel Band," which was a concert by the NIU Steelband.

The panel was a resounding success and despite its early morning time slot (8:30 a.m.) was well attended. With a wealth of positive feedback from his paper presentation in tow, Rossing was able to refine his research paper into a scholarly article that was later published in 1996 in the journal *Physics Today* under the title "Music from Oil Drums: The Acoustics of Steel Pan."[20] For their part, the performance, lecture, and demonstration at the ASA conference represented something much larger for O'Connor, Alexis, and the NIU Steelband. They were pushing the scientific boundaries of the steelpan and elevating the global respect and acceptance of the instrument. This was an important moment in Alexis's steelpan career as it marked a moment when the scientific community, using pragmatic methods, was able to explain and marvel at something invented by panmen in the neighborhoods of Trinidad and Tobago decades earlier. If the scientists of the ASA were interested in studying the science of the steelpan, surely it belonged in the academy of NIU and elsewhere as a serious instrument of study.

The success of Rossing and the NIU steelband program at the ASA conference in 1995 reached beyond the United States, and word of their research and discoveries reached Trinidad and Tobago in early 1996. Inspired by the findings of the NIU steelpan researchers, the first International Conference on the Science and Technology of the Steelpan (ICSTS) was held in Trinidad during the World Steelband Music Festival in 2000. The conference was jointly sponsored by Pan Trinbago (an influential Trinidadian steelband organization) and the National Institute of Higher Education, Research,

Science and Technology (NIHERST) and featured international scientists, technologists, tuners, and steelpan makers from the United States, Switzerland, France, Japan, Canada, and the Caribbean.[21] Alexis and Rossing were among the invited presenters at the conference, and their research was well received, further elevating the esteem of steelpan in the United States.

CHAPTER 7

PANNING TO THE EAST—THE NIU STEELBAND CAPTURES ASIA

The East Coast tours of the 1970s, the trips to PASIC, and the performance and demonstration at the Acoustical Society in 1995 served to bolster the reputation and status of the NIU steelband program. O'Connor and Alexis spent the better part of the 1980s slowly earning the respect of the Trinidadian public and steelpan community. But it was two highly successful tours to Taiwan in 1992 and 1998 and a tour to South Korea to perform at the 2002 World Cup and the fourth annual Seoul Drum Festival that solidified the NIU Steelband's international reputation.

Upon returning from a visit to Trinidad in 1957, American folk musician and political icon Pete Seeger announced that steelpan "was destined to spread to the farthest reaches of the globe."[1] And indeed, the past half century has seen the sounds and spirit of steelpan infiltrate six continents and countless countries. In places such as Europe and North America, the inroads have been brisk, and in others, more gradual or not at all. Asia falls in the latter category. The continent saw small pockets of active, though isolated, steelband activity in Japan and Australia prior to the 1990s; however, these steelband scenes were not widespread, and Asia remains by and large a relatively recent conquest for the music of steelpan. Asia, the island of Taiwan included, had never before seen or heard the likes of the famous touring Trinidadian steelbands. Bands such as Amril's Cavaliers had previously toured Australia and gone to Hong Kong, but until 1988, Taiwan and mainland Asia were virtually untouched steelpan territory.

How and why was the NIU Steelband able to successfully tour Taiwan in 1992 and 1998? One need look no further than fellow NIU School of Music professor Kou-Huang Han for the spark and connection that led to open doors in Taiwan for the NIU Steelband. Despite earning a Ph.D. in musicology from Northwestern University, with a dissertation in Marian antiphons (early religious music from the Western European tradition), Han was an ethnomusicologist at heart, and through his upbringing in mainland China and Taiwan, he developed a deep love of Chinese and Indonesian traditional music.² He was hired as a musicologist to teach Western music history at NIU in 1974 and quickly took advantage of the open-mindedness of the faculty by starting an Indonesian gamelan and Chinese music ensemble. Han, like O'Connor, was much more interested in world music than in Western classical music and eventually was able, over time, to shift his teaching responsibilities away from the traditional Western canon to exclusively world music and ethnomusicology. According to Han, "The Music Department (not School yet) seemed very eager to accept new ideas. It was also one way to compete with other big universities in Illinois. 'We have something you don't have.' After all, they let me introduce world music from scratch even though I was hired to teach Western music history initially."³

Like Alexis's relationships to Trinidad and Tobago, Han kept very close contact with friends, family, and colleagues back in Taiwan, and he was eager to bring a group of his American students from NIU to Taiwan to perform. The opportunity came during the period from December 1978 to January 1979 when Han and the NIU Gamelan and Chinese Orchestra toured Taiwan and Hong Kong at the invitation of the Taiwanese government.⁴ The tour was a success, and the NIU Chinese Orchestra—billed at the time as the only Chinese orchestra in the world comprised of non-Chinese performers—made a very strong impression upon the government and academic institutions of Taiwan.⁵

In the mid-1980s, the president of the National Institute of the Arts in Taiwan, Professor Shui-Long Ma, came to visit Han in DeKalb. Professor Ma was a close friend of Han, and in addition to his administrative duties at the National Institute of the Arts in Taiwan, Ma is a well-known composer of contemporary Western European classical music.⁶ According to Han, Professor Ma was impressed by the diversity and quality of the NIU world music ensembles. "He [Ma] was amazed in seeing so many world-music-related activities at NIU and invited me to go to his school as a visiting professor to set up a similar program which was 'far out' then because people knew only Western and Chinese music."⁷ Ma returned to Taiwan with an eye and ear toward the future, and this future included building similar programs at the National Institute of the Arts in Taiwan. This was the beginning of the connection between NIU and the National Institute of the Arts in Taiwan (now known as Taipei National University of the Arts, hereafter TNUA).

During the academic year 1985–86, Han was awarded a sabbatical from his teaching duties at NIU and traveled to Taiwan in order to set up and begin teaching a gamelan ensemble at TNUA. The program was a huge success, and Han suggested to the TNUA administration that O'Connor and Alexis come to Taiwan in order to set up a similar program, this time with steelband as the main instrument of focus. The plan was approved by TNUA, and the NIU administration and Alexis and O'Connor were eager to travel east. Thus in the fall of 1988, O'Connor and Alexis set out for a Taiwanese adventure. For Alexis, this would be a short sojourn as he was only scheduled to be in Taiwan for two weeks, the time necessary to build the steelpans used by the new steelband. O'Connor, on the other hand, had taken a sabbatical from his duties at NIU and was scheduled to stay the entire school year at TNUA. Officially, the pair had been invited by the Taipei National University of the Arts to build steelpans and establish a steelband in an effort to expand the university's existing percussion program. Steelpan was truly exotic to most Taiwanese people, and it was with great excitement and curiosity that the people of Taiwan welcomed Alexis and O'Connor as they arrived and set up shop.

After two weeks of pounding, burning, sinking, and tapping, the instruments were finished, Alexis flew home, and O'Connor set about teaching steelband and conducting rehearsals with his new ensemble. The TNUA steelband was the first steelband of its kind in Taiwan, and at nearly every concert the band played for people hearing steelpan for the first time. The modest size of the band notwithstanding (there were only six sets of steelpans plus a drum set), the band was a huge success. Midway through the academic year 1988–1989, O'Connor was summoned back to DeKalb due to a family emergency. As he hastily made arrangements to return home, the steelband program he had just spent the past semester fostering was in limbo without a suitable replacement for the director's position. Taipei National University of the Arts, however, was hooked on steelpan and, not wanting the program to languish, set about finding a permanent replacement for the departing panman in order to lead the band and keep the steelpan music alive. TNUA, O'Connor, and Alexis turned to one of their top steelpan students back at NIU for the job.

Like Jeannine Remy before her and Liam Teague after, Sarah Barnes-Tsai was a protégé student of O'Connor and Alexis at Northern Illinois University and had earned undergraduate and graduate degrees in percussion at the institution. Unlike Remy and Teague, Barnes-Tsai was very interested in Asian music and was a graduate assistant of Professor Han at NIU. She was, in addition to steelpan, an accomplished gamelan and hammer dulcimer performer, and in the final stages of completing a world-music graduate degree in 1989 when TNUA came calling with the offer of a teaching position.[8] Eager for an adventure, Barnes-Tsai accepted the offer and arrived in Taiwan in the spring of 1989 on what she thought was a six-month contract to fill O'Connor's previous position teaching steelpan. The experience for Barnes-Tsai was decidedly different from O'Connor's: whereas O'Connor had a full-time translator and an assortment of personal assistants, Barnes-Tsai had neither translators nor assistants and had to fend for herself.[9] Regardless of the barriers in front of her, Barnes-Tsai flourished in the position, and upon the expiration of the contract at the end of the semester, a full-time position was created and Barnes-Tsai was hired permanently to teach steelpan, percussion, and academic courses in music—a position she holds to this day (2017).[10]

With the connections of Han, O'Connor, Alexis, and now Sarah Barnes-Tsai firmly established in Taiwan, NIU and TNUA would enjoy a reciprocal relationship over the next several years. One such partnership was with percussion professor Tzong-Ching Ju of TNUA, who in 1990 took a year-long leave of absence to serve as music director of the National Concert Hall in Taiwan.[11] In addition to his duties at TNUA, Professor Ju was the founder and director of a nationally famous professional performing group: the

Ju Percussion group. Professor Ju began his percussion group in 1986, and they quickly became influential in the Taiwan arts scene. Barnes-Tsai worked closely with Professor Ju at TNUA, and it was at the behest of Professor Ju and the Ju Percussion group that the NIU Steelband was invited to come to Taiwan in May of 1991.[12] Professor Ju was involved in the planning process of the Taipei International Percussion Festival held in 1993, and he was interested in the support and publicity that the NIU Steelband could bring to TNUA and the Ju Percussion group.[13]

In the spring of 1991, O'Connor and Professor Ju began serious negotiations, and on May 7, the NIU Steelband was officially invited by the Ju Percussion Foundation to come to Taiwan and perform throughout the country.[14] The NIU Steelband was engaged for several performances at universities around Taiwan, and the National Theater and Concert Hall of Taiwan arranged for two marquee concerts. In addition to the concerts and performances, the Ju Percussion Group was particularly interested in having NIU faculty members O'Connor, Chappell, and Holly give lectures and demonstrations on various aspects of classical and world percussion.

O'Connor knew that the trip was a great opportunity to gain exposure internationally for the NIU Steelband, but he was much more concerned about the students and their wellbeing. For many, this would be their first trip outside the United States, and O'Connor worried about culture shock. Alexis further exacerbated the situation by telling terrorizing stories regarding the cuisine; he claimed that he could not find fried chicken during his time in Taiwan in 1988. According to Barnes-Tsai, when Alexis was in Taiwan in 1988 to build steelpans for TNUA, he "did the sinking and tuning in a matter of only 3 or 4 days. In the evenings we would go to the American part of Taipei (Tien Mu), to a restaurant called Jake's and get... a nice chicken dinner or other Western types of food."[15] In order to combat anxieties over dietary needs, O'Connor made arrangements to serve American-style breakfast at the hostel in which the NIU students were staying during their time in Taiwan.[16] The financial aspect of the trip was another burden that O'Connor had to remedy. In his opinion, students pay tuition to attend NIU, and he felt strongly that an activity—such as this trip to Taiwan—should not cost the students extra. "I told Cliff and the Dean of the College of Visual and Performing Arts that this Taiwan thing can't cost the students a dime."[17]

O'Connor and Alexis quickly realized, however, that funding the trip to Taiwan was more complicated than originally anticipated. Part of the initial agreement was that the Ju Percussion Foundation agreed to pay for the hotel, food, and transportation accommodations of the NIU Steelband while in Taiwan. They also agreed to pay for the air cargo charges to bring the steelpan and equipment to Taiwan and half the airfare for the students and faculty. In total, twenty-five persons from NIU embarked on the trip, twenty students and five faculty members (O'Connor, Alexis, Chappell, Holly, and Han, who accompanied the band and served as a translator and liaison). This meant that O'Connor and Alexis would be charged with paying for 50 percent of the airfare for twenty-five persons and transportation to and from Chicago O'Hare airport from DeKalb for the students and the equipment.

At the time, the NIU Steelband did not have any generous benefactors to shoulder the financial burden. The manner in which O'Connor, determined not to charge the students

FIGURE 7.1. NIU Steelband CSK Hall Performance, Taiwan (1992)

for the trip, secured the rest of the funding offers a fine example of his resourcefulness as an administrator. First, through O'Connor's request, the National Theater and Concert Hall of Taiwan agreed to pay the NIU Steelband an honorarium of $5,000 USD. He then secured funding from the College of Visual and Performing Arts and the NIU School of Music to pay for most of the student portion ($25,000), which was supplemented with funds from the NIU Steelband gig account (approximately $10,000). The balance of the fare was paid by means of a request that O'Connor made to the provost of graduate studies at NIU. Finally, the NIU Steelband shared in the concert sales revenue from the various venues of the tour. Two days before NIU was set to leave Taiwan, O'Connor met with Professor Ju. "He hands me 80 one hundred dollar US bills, and says, 'This is for you. That's your fees for all your concerts.' ... So I came back here with $8,000 not knowing if I was going to have anything. That's how we funded the first CD."[18]

In total, in addition to the funds supplied by the Taiwanese partners, O'Connor raised nearly $13,000 for the Taiwan trip and succeeded in funding the trip in full for the students and faculty members.[19] The overall trip cost was approximately $50,000, and the fact that this was funded in full was no small consolation for the efforts of all involved. With the funding secured, the Taiwan tour was approved by the NIU administration, and the NIU Steelband was set to tour the country from March 11 to March 22, 1992. The tour would later gather the co-sponsorship of the Coordination Council of North American Affairs wing of the Taiwanese government.[20] Local arrangements were made via the Ju Percussion Foundation. NIU professor Han served as a liaison and translator, and Sarah Barnes-Tsai served as another liaison and coordinator of many of the band's activities while on the tour.

TABLE 7.1. NIU STEELBAND TAIWAN TRIP ITINERARY, 1992

Date	Activity
3/11	NIU Steelband leaves Chicago O'Hare international Airport
3/12	Arrive in Taipei in the late evening
3/13	A.M. rehearsal for the steelband / P.M. Lecture "Style and Performances Practices: Drum Set—Rich Holly presenter
3/14	Rehearsal
3/15	Outdoor Concert Chaing Kai-Shek Memorial Square
3/16	Concert at National Concert Hall in Taipei
3/17	A.M. rehearsal for the steelband / P.M. Lecture "Caribbean and Latin American Music"—O'Connor and Chappell presenters
3/18	Lecture "African and Brazilian Music"—Holly and Chappell (with Han)/ Concert at Ching Hua University
3/19	Open
3/20	Concert in Taichung County
3/21	Concert in Tao-Yuan County
3/22	Leave Taipei and return to DeKalb

O'Connor, Alexis, and the organizers from the Ju Percussion Group understood from the outset of the tour that shipping all the instruments to Taiwan would be prohibitively expensive. With this in mind, Alexis was sent ahead of the rest of the NIU Steelband in order to make some of the steelpans needed for the performances; it was more economical to send the man rather than the drums—though in the end they ended up shipping two sets of bass steelpans for the tour. Per the agreement with the Ju Percussion Group and the TNUA, these steelpans were left in Taiwan upon the completion of the tour, and now comprise the basis for the steelbands of the Ju Percussion Group and the TNUA steelband.[21] During his first trip to Taiwan in 1988, Alexis's steelpan building went off without incident. He premade all the frontline steelpans and only needed to do the finishing tuning of the instruments once in Taiwan. The process of building the new steelpans in 1988 was smooth and relatively uneventful.

However, things did not go according to plan for the NIU tour in 1992, and Sarah Barnes-Tsai recalls that Alexis's bravado may have gotten the better of him:

> [This time] Cliff burned his hands with hydrochloric acid. He was washing the drums without gloves (much to my shock and dismay!). He said he was used to it. Unfortunately, the acid here was a stronger percentage, and the poor man called me early the next day in great pain! We went to MacKay Hospital for assistance but they only gave him some cream.
>
> Some assistant from Mr. Ju's group took him to another hospital that evening, and they were able to wash his hands in some solution, gave him pain killers and better salve. What an

ordeal. I had only been in Taiwan for three years so my spoken Chinese wasn't great. And I didn't own a car yet so we needed to depend on taxis for transportation.[22]

The ordeal did little to stifle his spirits and, working eighteen-hour days, Alexis completed the entire set of steelpans from start to finish in four days. A testament to his skills as a builder and tuner, the original steelpans built for TNUA in 1988 were still in great shape and needed very little tuning and blending to fit in with the new ones.[23]

The NIU Steelband tour to Taiwan had several official purposes, one of which was education. With this in mind, the NIU faculty members gave a number of scholarly lectures on world-music topics for the students of TNUA, Ching Hua University, Ju Percussion members, and the general public. Other official purposes of the Taiwan tour (the goodwill and university exposure quotient) were seemingly secondary to the educational mission, and the lectures on various musical topics (see chart above) further offered O'Connor and Alexis the educational impetus to justify the trip to the NIU administration.

The marquee performance of the tour was held at the Chiang Kai-Shek National Concert Hall in Taipei for an audience in excess of 3,000 people. Unsure of Taiwanese sensibilities, O'Connor and Alexis were cautiously optimistic regarding their choice of repertoire for the performance. The enthusiastic reception the band had received thus far on the tour was reassuring, but how would the Taiwanese react to something more traditional and perhaps less accessible—say, a Trinidadian-style road march or calypso? O'Connor told several newspapers after the fact, "I was apprehensive when we left the National Theater, wondering if the Taiwanese would accept the authentic calypsos we played. The classical (Bach, Barber, Bizet) was well-accepted, but they went nuts over the calypsos. . . . They wouldn't let us stop until we ran out of pieces!"[24] The NIU Steelband's concerts and performances represented a first hearing of steelpan for most of the Taiwanese, something completely new. They were open vessels, and considering the uniqueness of steelpan, the NIU Steelband may as well have arrived on a spaceship.

Although his fears turned out to be unfounded, choosing the band's repertoire for the Taiwan tour in 1992 was a careful process on which O'Connor and Alexis expended a great deal of energy. Every attempt was made to balance the full spectrum of available steelband repertoire from classical to calypso to pop tunes. After much deliberation O'Connor and Alexis settled on the set list noted in Table 7.2.

TABLE 7.2. CONCERT REPERTOIRE, TAIWAN TOUR, 1992

Say it with Pan	Cliff Alexis
Toccata and Fugue in d minor	J.S. Bach, arr. Al O'Connor
I Can't Wait Another Minute	The High Five, arr. Cliff Alexis
Wood-N-Steel	Robert Chappell
Intermission	
Pan Dingolay	Lord Kitchener, arr. Cliff Alexis
Adagio	Samuel Barber, arr. Al O'Connor

Confusion	Cliff Alexis
Have You Seen Her?	The Chi-Lites, arr. Cliff Alexis
Fire Down Below	Len "Boogsie" Sharpe

The selections were chosen to showcase the talents of the NIU Steelband and to display to an uninitiated audience the possibilities, masterwork triumphs, and various genre traditions of steelband music. Other selections were chosen to represent the history of the NIU Steelband and its geographic location in the United States—ergo, "Have You Seen Her?" the hit soul song by the Chi-Lites.

Regardless, the repertoire was, by order of the Taiwanese government, sent ahead of time for preapproval by the Coordination Council of North American Affairs and the Ju Percussion Group. Lost in translation—literally and figuratively—the Trinidadian dialect of English that is so common and an inextricable a part of Trinidadian music and its calypso roots was a sticking point for Taiwanese officials. In particular, the word "Dingolay" from the piece "Pan Dingolay" and the song title "Fire Down Below" were particularly troubling. According to Shu-Kang Liu of the Ju Percussion Group, "First, there is a piece named 'Pan Dingolay' in your repertoire. We do not quite understand what does the word 'Dingolay' mean. Also, could you further explain the meaning of 'Fire Down Below?'"[25] Seemingly concerned about the possible revolutionary or suggestive nature of the terms, they seemed fine once they learned that "Dingolay" described a dance style. The latter is a masterwork of composer Len "Boogsie" Sharpe, a legendary figure in Trinidad. As leader and arranger of the Trinidadian steelband Phase II, the mercurial Sharpe is one of the most beloved and influential figures in steelband today. The title, "Fire Down Below" has a long history in Trinidad and Tobago, notably as the title of a very popular 1957 film shot in Trinidad starring Rita Hayworth, Jack Lemmon, and Robert Mitchum. The song has served as a popular tune to arrange ever since it first charted in 1957—via the American jazz singer Jeri Southern—as the title track to the film.[26]

Perhaps the most unique piece of repertoire performed during the tour was "Wood-n-Steel," written by NIU faculty member Robert Chappell. The piece was penned specially for the tour and melded African, Caribbean, and American music traditions. According to Robert Chappell, "O'Connor came to me and said, 'We've got this great tour going to Taiwan. I want you to write a piece for it, and of course you have to learn how to play the pan, cause you have to play in the band.'"[27] In particular, "Wood-n-Steel" is a fusion of the Ugandan Amadinda xylophone tradition and the steelband tradition of Trinidad and Tobago. Chappell based the rhythmic and melodic material of the composition on the traditional Amadinda work "Omujooni: Balinserekerera Balinsala ekyamb." "Wood-n-Steel" evolves gradually and employs metric modulation to move through its various cycles. Chappell was interested in developing multiple independent ostinatos (common in African Amadinda music) with the frantic theme and variation development so common to Trinidadian steelband music.[28] The result is a work unlike any other in the steelband canon, which adeptly showcased the range of the NIU Steelband in the realm of steelband and beyond. "Wood-n-Steel" was a crowd-pleaser for the Taiwanese, and would later go on to become one of the band's signature pieces, wowing audiences at NIU and in Trinidad during the World Steelband Music Festival competition in 2000.[29] Moreover, the Amadinda xylophone that the NIU Steelband brought with them to Taiwan was given as a gift to the Ju Percussion Group by the NIU Steelband as a token of appreciation for organizing the tour and their generous hospitality.

For many members of the NIU Steelband, the 1992 Taiwan tour was their first trip outside the United States, a maiden voyage. Yet for nearly all the tour participants, even those from the Caribbean or with some international experience, the food and culture of Taiwan was a life-changing experience. O'Connor had arranged for American-style breakfast to be served every morning at the hostel where the band was lodged, but much to his surprise the students immediately embraced the local fare. One particularly adventurous group of students told O'Connor, "We found a guy around the corner who makes fried squid skin, and it's great!"[30] Throughout the course of the tour, the NIU Steelband enjoyed meals served family style, with numerous Taiwanese students sitting among the NIU students in order translate, help deal with the newness of the food options, and affect cultural exchange on an informal level. Taiwanese hospitality greatly impressed the NIU Steelband members on the tour.

If the NIU Steelband members were not fully aware of Taiwanese culture and cuisine, the Taiwanese were indeed fully aware of the NIU Steelband, and the concerts of the tour were generously promoted in local newspapers, flyers, and posters around the city. A small group of NIU Steelband members even performed on a popular Taiwanese variety showed called *Hit or Miss*.[31] The lavishly decorated concert posters became a regular sight around town, and as Lana Wardell recalls, "Everywhere we went, there were big posters in bright red and black promoting the concert."[32] The Ju Percussion Group and TNUA had arranged for Taiwanese students to travel and intermingle with the NIU students in an effort for cultural exchange and to ease the culture shock. In addition to Professor Han, O'Connor and Alexis had Taiwanese translators, aides, and liaisons to guide them through the tour. Even with a large contingent of support, the NIU Steelband members were not ready for the excitement and royal treatment they received from the Taiwanese public. Autographs are not something student steelbands are accustomed to giving, and according to band member Julie Stephens, "Every time we turned around, someone was holding out a flyer and a pen."[33]

Alexis and O'Connor anticipated raising funds for the NIU steelband program after the tour by recording an album of the pieces performed on the Taiwan tour. However, once in Taiwan Alexis and O'Connor were pleased to discover that the National Concert Hall was well equipped for live recording. With the help of National Concert Hall director Professor Ju, the NIU Steelband recorded its concert set from the live performance on March 16, 1992. The nine arrangements (listed above) recorded on the album included the crowd favorites "Wood-n-Steel" and "Fire Down Below." The album was produced and released by the NIU School of Music and, like the NIU Steelband's earlier studio album *N.I.U. Steel Band Plays Calypso-Pop-Classics* released in 1976, was sold at concerts, gigs, and performances to generate funds in support of the NIU steelband program.

Return to Taiwan, 1998

Following the NIU Steelband's tour to Taiwan in 1992, the Taiwanese love of steelpan was set; they had been bitten by the pan jumbie. The impact of the tour was great, and the NIU Steelband was asked back to Taiwan in 1998 for another tour. This time, however, the tour took on a decidedly different tone from the first tour in 1992. For the 1998 tour O'Connor and Alexis brought a larger band (thirty students and faculty) than in 1992 (twenty-five students and faculty), and the tour was scheduled to be longer (two full weeks) with more concerts (nine, in contrast to just four in 1992). The tour was once again sponsored by the Ju Percussion Foundation, who agreed to pay the airfare for the NIU Steelband members. However, despite another scheduled performance at the National Concert Hall, the NIU Steelband would not be paid for the performance and needed to lean heavily on the NIU Foundation and steelband patron Lester Trilla to pay the balance of the costs.[34]

According to NIU officials, this was the first time a student performing group of any kind had been invited back to Taiwan for an encore performance.[35] The NIU Steelband's 1998 Taiwan tour began with high aspirations; after all, the 1992 tour had been wildly successful, and for the 1998 tour the NIU Steelband was again polished and ready for the task at hand. A mid-March travel date was again chosen for the tour to maximize the travel itinerary without disrupting the student class schedules too greatly by taking advantage of NIU's spring break. As such, the tour was scheduled to take place from March 10 to March 20. But things were different from the very start of the tour. First, the tour was delayed by one day due to a massive snowstorm that closed Chicago's O'Hare International Airport on March 10. Because of this delay, the marquee National Concert Hall concert was cancelled, much to the disappointment of NIU students and faculty.

Whereas the 1992 Taiwan tour had featured the hospitality of a plethora of TNUA students aiding the NIU steelband in their endeavors, the 1998 tour was not privy to the same Taiwanese student involvement and hospitality. This was due in part to the concert schedule, which featured performances at mostly public institutions in rural counties outside the capital city of Taipei, such as the Chih-Shan Sport Park and Gan-Shan Concert Hall.[36] Further, the 1998 tour did not include the same scholarly lectures from NIU percussion faculty. In 1998, Holly and Han did not accompany the band, and Alexis, Chappell, and O'Connor were completely focused on rehearsals and performances of the NIU Steelband without the engagement of public lectures. It is worth noting that the 1998 version of the NIU Steelband did feature the then-young student Liam Teague who, unsurprisingly, amazed the Taiwanese public with his virtuosity and musicianship.

The repertoire chosen for the 1998 tour was equally challenging and no less impressive than that of the 1992 tour. A balance of Latin, calypso, classical, and American popular tunes comprised the set list, which was arranged by O'Connor and Alexis. Highlights of the selections included well-polished version of George Frideric Handel's *Water Music* and two Panorama style arrangements—"Mind Yuh Business" and "Misbehave"—by Len "Boogsie" Sharpe. Replacing the highly successful "Wood-n-Steel" from the 1992 Taiwan concert tour was another Robert Chappell composition, "Variations Brasileiras," another experimental composition that blended non-Trinidadian musical traditions (this time the Brazilian "IIe Aiye" and bateria drumming) with steelband.[37]

A retrospective look at the 1998 tour suggests that it was not as impactful as the 1992 tour; nonetheless, the performances of the 1998 tour were still a huge success, and the band received standing ovations and endless calls for encores at every tour stop. The band received star treatment from Taiwanese supporters, and according to Thomas Hapeman, "Even though they've never heard the music before, we were adored as rock stars" and the tour met with great success.[38]

Once again, a major tour became the impetus to make an album, and *Return to Taiwan* became the NIU Steelband's third album. The album was recorded and produced by NIU percussion faculty Robert Chappell and self-released by the NIU School of Music. The album's repertoire mirrored that of the 1998 Taiwan tour repertoire and included such titles as "Generation Concerto" written by O'Connor's son Ethan O'Connor and featuring Teague as soloist, "Mind Yuh Business," several other Latin numbers and calypsos, and a medley of Taiwanese folk songs. The international reputation of the NIU Steelband was again furthered by the 1998 Taiwan tour, and just as they had in 1992, columnists and opinion-page writers in Trinidadian newspapers bristled over the success of the NIU steelband in Taiwan.[39] An American steelband had, once again, beaten Trinidadian steelbands in the race to spread steelpan around the globe.

Korea World Cup 2002

In May of 2002, the NIU Steelband returned to Asia. The band was invited by the city officials of Seoul, South Korea, to participate in the fourth annual Seoul Drum Festival. Usually held in September or October, the 2002 Seoul Drum Festival was pushed forward to May to coincide with the 2002 FIFA World Cup. In a decisive stroke of economic strength and civic pride, Seoul had been chosen (along with Japan) to host the 2002 FIFA World Cup. This was the first time an Asian country had hosted the event, and Korea and Japan jumped at the opportunity to showcase their countries and cultures to a vast global audience while the World Cup was going on.

The Seoul Drum Festival was founded in 1999 to bring together Eastern and Western cultures and music to a unifying theme, "Beat it! Enjoy it! Feel it!" With the opportunity of the influx of peoples from around the globe descending on Seoul for the World Cup, the Seoul Drum Festival made plans for the biggest festival of its brief history. City leaders spent millions of dollars on events that promoted Korean music, culture, and heritage—and the Seoul Drum Festival was one such beneficiary. In all, 32 teams from around the globe qualified for the World Cup Finals, and the 2002 Seoul Drum Festival narrowed its participants to one representative group from each of the countries participating in the World Cup. The NIU Steelband was chosen to represent the United States.

Putting aside the irony that a steelband was representing the United States and not Trinidad and Tobago (which did not qualify for the 2002 World Cup), how exactly the NIU

Steelband was chosen to represent the United States is a peculiar story in itself. In early 2001, Seoul Drum Festival organizers contacted the Percussive Arts Society and asked for recommendations of "professional" ensembles to represent the United States at the festival. President Jim Campbell of the Percussive Arts Society enthusiastically recommended the NIU Steelband. Campbell was an NIU graduate, having earned both a bachelor's and a master's degree in percussion performance at the institution in the 1970s, and he was one of the founding members of the NIU Steelband in the 1970s. According to Campbell, "There's no more professional group than the one from NIU. They have the highest professional standards, and I know this is as professional as it gets. People recognize it as a premier program, O'Connor has been a driving force in steelband and one of the most respected music educators in the U.S."[40]

For O'Connor, the timing of the invitation came as a bit of a shock and was accompanied with an underlying feeling of trepidation. The NIU Steelband had just returned from their triumphant second-place finish at the World Steelband Music Festival in Trinidad during the fall of 2000. Having just spent their funds on the Trinidad trip, the NIU Steelband was broke, and O'Connor was exhausted. O'Connor and Alexis were flattered by the invitation—it was a true honor—however, both men knew the magnitude of such an endeavor. The band would be ready to play—this was the easy part—but the prospect of engaging in yet another Asian tour was daunting financially and administratively. Savvy businessman that he was, O'Connor communicated an ultimatum to the festival organizers, "You pay for everything door-to-door, including instrument freight, and we'll come." A few days later, the festival organizers in conjunction with the mayor of Seoul sent confirmation of an all-expense-paid trip for three faculty and twenty students. As a result of the funding restrictions, O'Connor and Alexis had to cut down the size of the NIU Steelband and choose only certain members to join the trip. O'Connor commented, "There were very happy students, and some not so happy."[41]

This trip would be unlike the other international tours to Taiwan in that the NIU Steelband would only perform at the Seoul Drum Festival, the opening ceremonies for the World Cup, and two other small performances. In contrast to the aggressive schedules of the Taiwan tours, the Korea tour offered more time for students to explore the city and take in the spectacle of the World Cup. Adam Grise noted that the NIU Steelband performed in different venues all around Seoul, each time paired with a different group, including a dinner in which the band played for international dignitaries assembled for the World Cup.[42] The NIU Steelband was received warmly at the World Cup opening ceremonies, and their performances at the Seoul Drum Festival went swimmingly.

With the exception of Japan, which has an increasingly vibrant steelband scene, Asia has been slow in taking up steelbands, and the NIU Steelband appearances were key in bringing further exposure for the band and the instrument in Asia. This is especially true of Taiwan, where the efforts of the NIU Steelband helped establish and develop a local steelpan movement.

FIGURE 7.2. NIU Steelband performing at Seoul Drum Festival, Korea (2002)

CHAPTER 8

THE PAGANINI OF PAN, LIAM TEAGUE, COMES TO NIU

> Sir, right now in my life I've got no idea what I am going to do because honestly, if I don't get into university, I think within the next couple of years I think I may be on the streets.
> —Liam Teague to Al O'Connor (1992)[1]

The year 1989 was good for O'Connor, Alexis, and the NIU Steelband. O'Connor's career, in particular, took a major turn for the better. During the late summer he was promoted to the position of Associate Dean of the College of Performing and Visual Arts at NIU. In addition to his duties with the NIU Steelband, O'Connor was now in charge of monitoring academic programs, coordinating academic reviews, preparing budgets, tracking student performance data and student recruitment, and supervising financial aid and scholarships.[2] With his new position came great responsibility, and O'Connor's seemingly nonexistent time was now stretched even further. He nonetheless found plenty of time to play steelpan and retained his duties as steelband co-director.

In November of that same year, O'Connor undertook yet another step in his lifelong steelpan journey, embarking on his first visit to Trinidad and Tobago. This was the very first trip to the birthplace of steelpan for O'Connor, and he was eager to take in the sights, sounds, and smells of the place to whose musical culture he was so devoted. Alexis had been singing the praises of his NIU colleague to the panmen of Trinidad and Tobago for some time and was eager to take O'Connor to the panyards and introduce him to the legends and pioneers of the craft. For Alexis, the trip was less about a homecoming and more about establishing the credibility of O'Connor and NIU in the circles of influential government and Pan Trinbago officials. The international success of the NIU steelband program would need to start, first and foremost, in Trinidad and Tobago, and Alexis called upon his own personal reputation as a nationally respected steelpan legend to put weight behind the NIU Steelband and its director. Little did O'Connor and Alexis know that their trip to Trinidad in 1989 would have such important lasting ramifications for the steelband program at NIU, as this was the trip in which O'Connor and Alexis first met steelpan prodigy and future NIU steelband faculty member Liam Teague.

In July of 1989, O'Connor and Alexis were officially invited by Selwyn Tarradath of Pan Trinbago to come to Trinidad and Tobago as special guests of the organization.[3] Tarradath was the education officer of Pan Trinbago, an original member of the famous Woodbrook steelband Phase II, and a lifelong friend of Alexis. By 1989, the name Al O'Connor was a familiar one to many Trinidadian steelpan enthusiasts, as his arrangement of Aaron Copland's *Appalachian Spring* was performed to rave reviews by the Our Boys Steel Orchestra during the 1988 Pan Is Beautiful steelband competition.

Trinidad and Tobago has a biannual nationwide festival held in the fall that celebrates steelband beyond the scope of Carnival. The festival is divided by age group, with a youth competition and an adult competition. The two competitions are held in even/odd year cycles. The youth competition is called the National Schools Steelband Festival, and the adult competition is known as Pan Is Beautiful. Through Alexis's influence and lobbying Pan Trinbago became interested in having O'Connor as a judge for the biannual National Schools Steelband Competition. Trinidad and Tobago is no stranger to having outsiders and non-panmen judge steelband competitions. In fact, many of the early steelband competitions in the 1950s were judged, in part, by British music educators, who had very little or no background in steelband.[4] Further, the very first Trinidadian Panorama steelband competition held in 1963 was judged by Captain John McDonald, a US Navy officer and musician who was the Chief Naval Officer of the US military base in Chaguaramas, Trinidad from 1961 to 1963.[5] In this sense, O'Connor's judging of Pan Is Beautiful in 1989 was part of a larger tradition. Throughout the years, many winners of the steelpan soloist competition from the National Schools Steelband Festival have gone on to great things in steelpan, such as solo careers or established careers as arrangers. O'Connor was to judge the finals of the competition as a guest judge and comment on the overall process of the festival adjudication. His scores were not counted toward the final tally, nor were his comments made public. The Trinidadian school steelbands used many of the same arrangers as the adult steelbands, and O'Connor raved that "the standard and the level of playing is quite high."[6]

O'Connor judged the bands and soloists the way *he* thought best and felt right at home with the score sheet and rubric for assessing performers created by Pan Trinbago.[7] The original Pan Trinbago score sheets assessed elements such as "tuning" and "blend," which O'Connor felt antithetical to the overall success of a given steelband "These are kids who play. How are we supposed to penalize them for a bad tuning job? They had nothing to do with that."[8] But in all, O'Connor's judging for this competition (and later for Pan Is Beautiful in 1992) was praised for its in-depth comments, knowledge, and understanding of steelpan and steelband music. According to O'Connor, "Many of the panmen have said that it is the European and American judges who really don't know what they are listening to. Many of the comments they write are based upon the way an orchestra would play the classical piece. When they get to a calypso, they are totally dumbfounded. After some of the steelbands read my preliminary sheets, they were surprised I knew their nomenclature. I talked about the strum patterns; I called the instruments by their proper names and suggested different ways of orchestrating parts, etc.; I made useful comments which the bands tried to polish."[9]

The finals of the National Schools Steelband Festival competition were held in the Jean Pierre complex in Port of Spain. The complex is designed as a sports stadium with seating for approximately 6,000 spectators and is normally at or near capacity for the festival competition. However, for this year's competition the attendance was drastically low, in the range of 2500. Rumors swirled in the Trinidadian press over the low attendance and the reasons for it, though popular consensus was that the country was still riding a wave of depression stemming from the lost World Cup Soccer qualifying match between the United States and Trinidad and Tobago national teams. The United States won the match on Paul Caligiuri's scintillating "shot heard 'round the world."[10] The match was held on November 19, six days before the finals of the steelband competition; yet, the agony of defeat was still apparently all-consuming for the rank-and-file citizens of Trinidad and Tobago, and as a result the audience of the National Schools Steelband Festival competition was comprised mainly of competition steelbands and their families.

The low attendance of the festival did not go unnoticed by the Trinidadian media. *Trinidad Express* columnist David Abdulah was particularly outspoken in his November 27, 1989 column titled "More respect for school pan festival," where he scolded the public, noting that "I don't think the football can explain the dismal turnout" and later that "this [attendance] is an extremely disappointing response and is not the kind of public support that should be given to the nation's youth who are our finest musicians."[11] Others, such as Selwyn Tarradath, during his address at the competition finals, likened the low audience turnout to a larger issue related to the instrument in Trinidad and Tobago—that the plight of steelband is similar to prophets not being honored in their own country.[12] Tarradath also used the opportunity to plug the accomplishments of O'Connor and the NIU steelband program, noting that "the University of Northern Illinois in the United States was offering a bachelor of arts degree in steelband music" and universities in Trinidad and Tobago were not offering such a degree.[13]

Attendance issues aside, the quality of the playing was spectacular, and O'Connor and Alexis were impressed with the school steelbands of Trinidad and Tobago. However, it was the solo competition in which the true genius of Trinidad and Tobago revealed itself. As O'Connor recalls, "I'd never seen such superb playing from students before."[14] As the rounds progressed from prelims to semifinals to finals, the cream rose to the top, and a handful of elite soloists were left standing to perform on the grand stage of the Jean Pierre stadium. Despite a wealth of talented soloists, one performance in particular caught the attention of both O'Connor and Alexis. O'Connor starred his judging sheet by the player he thought best, and this player was a young fifteen-year-old from San Fernando named Liam Teague. "When I heard Liam, oh my God! I had a list of names of the six or seven top players and right next to them I put numbers: Liam Teague, number one!"[15]

Despite his young age, Teague displayed blazing technique and refined musicianship. O'Connor was equally impressed by the composition skills of the young pannist as he effortlessly executed his own composition, "A Visit to Hell," for the judges during the competition's final round. Teague was a steelpan savant who begun playing the instrument at a relatively later age but progressed rapidly. By the time he met O'Connor and Alexis, Teague was a regular, performing with adult San Fernando steelbands. He began playing steelpan at the age of twelve in San Fernando, some thirty miles south of the capital of Port of Spain. Teague got into steelpan through the Cub Scouts. "I was introduced to the steelpan by a fellow Cub Scout, who was in my dad's Cub Scout troop, Darren Sheppard. Darren is a wonderful soloist and arranger and, at the time, played with the VAT19 Fonclaire Steelband in San Fernando. He brought an instrument to one of our meetings."[16]

Teague's fascination with the steelpan was immediate, and he joined his first steelband, the T&Tec Motown Steelband in San Fernando, shortly thereafter. It was here, with the T&Tec Motown Steelband, that Teague first learned to play the steelpan. Interestingly, the process was anything but easy for the future virtuoso. "I did not take to the pan with ease; it was actually extremely difficult for me. But, because of my almost obsessive work ethic (I never wanted to take bathroom breaks!), I started to develop quickly. Those early days were very challenging as many onlookers, and even band mates, didn't really believe I had any potential."[17]

Like most Trinidadian-born pannists, Teague began his steelpan education in the panyard, learning by rote. However, prior to starting the steelpan, Teague was already learning the recorder in high school and was introduced to the basics of reading music before ever entering the panyard. Teague benefited from his formal classical music training and was soon able to complement his rote learning with competency in Western classical music notation and harmony. Teague's father, Russell, was a classical music fan, and the great masters—Bach, Beethoven, Mozart—played on weekends at the Teague home over the airwaves of BBC Classical radio. This was an important influence for Teague, who started listening to, and appreciating, classical music from an early age. He discovered an early love for virtuoso violinists of the caliber of Jascha Heifetz and Itzhak Perlman, and was inspired to take up the instrument, eventually becoming quite proficient. This early love of classical music set him on a different path from the vast majority of contemporary Trinidadian pannists and countless soca-loving Trinidadian youths.

Located in the southwest of Trinidad, San Fernando is an industrial city with an economic base closely tied to the volatility of international petroleum markets; it is close to the nearby Point Lisas petroleum complex. As such, the city often experiences drastic bouts of unemployment and has historically struggled, like much of Trinidad and Tobago, with substandard living conditions for many residents. Issues with alcohol and drug use further plagued the area. Growing up in one of the poorer neighborhoods in San Fernando, Teague sought to use music as a means of escape. Despite the awful conditions, Teague was determined to use these challenges as motivation.

For example, in their judging for the 1989 solo competition, O'Connor and Alexis noted the refined tone and touch of Teague, a point for which he is particularly well known today. How did he develop such a mature skill at such a tender age? "Growing up, I lived next door to a man who was involved with drugs and alcohol. He would be up all night wining and slept all day. I practiced for hours and hours each day and if I practiced too loudly he would wake up and threaten to beat me and smash my pan. So I took it upon myself to develop the best tone while playing very fast and very softy so not to wake the neighbor."[18] Teague transcended these struggles, winning a number of steelpan solo competitions throughout Trinidad. His love of classical music led him to eventually join the Trinidad and Tobago Youth Orchestra, where he continued his serious study of the violin and further embarked on the path of becoming a well-rounded musician. Teague's fascination with violin music greatly influenced his original compositions for the solo steelpan as well. One of the defining moments of Teague's early career in steelpan came at the age of eighteen, when he was the co-winner of the National Steelband Music Festival soloist category, playing his own virtuosic composition, the violin-like "A Visit To Hell."

O'Connor and Alexis knew nothing of Teague's background; nonetheless, they were captivated by the skill and musicianship displayed during his performance at the National Schools competition. Upon meeting the young pannists after the conclusion of the competition, they were taken by Teague's gracious and unassuming personality. Teague had won the competition in 1989 (he would again win it in 1991), and an impressed O'Connor gave him a business card with contact information. As O'Connor remembers, "He said he wanted to come to the US and study, and I said sure, sure, thinking nothing of it at the time because a lot of people asked me that."[19] Alexis, O'Connor, and Teague would go their separate ways after this meeting, and it would be years before the two sides would once again cross paths.

By 1992 Teague won several more competitions, and his reputation as a steelpan soloist in Trinidad spread widely. Yet his tenacity as a performer and his countless accolades did not translate into financial prosperity. Teague grappled with the poor financial prospects of his future in Trinidad and Tobago. Mulling over what few options he had, Teague remembered his conversations with O'Connor and Alexis in 1989, and reached out with the proverbial shot in the dark. At the time, NIU was the only institution in the world to offer a college degree in steelpan, and Teague wrote an emotional letter to O'Connor, begging for admission and pleading his case for a better future. As Teague recalls, the situation was dire and his plea sincere: "I said that if I stayed in Trinidad too long, I didn't know what would become of me, that I probably would be a vagrant on the streets after a while."[20]

Teague loves his homeland and continues to this day on a relentless quest to promote the music and culture of Trinidad and Tobago around the globe. However, in 1992 Teague was unsure how to facilitate his future goals if he stayed in Trinidad and Tobago. The letter from Teague to O'Connor, dated May 20, 1992, read, "Sir, my main reason in writing this letter is in one phrase TO BEG YOU! I am desperate to get into your institution. You see, I am not one to rate up myself, but I think my accomplishments speak for themselves. I know that you've visited Trinidad and that you've seen the situation in this country."[21] In the passionate words of a desperate eighteen-year-old, Teague would go on to say, "Sir, right now in my life I've got no idea what I'm going to do because honestly if I don't get into university I think within the next couple of years I may be on the streets because at present people regard me as a musical prodigy but as I get older my career as a soloist will be over because I won't have my youth anymore. Mr. O'Connor I'm begging you Please! Please! Help me get out of this country."[22] Years later, Teague fondly recalls the letter and admits that he somewhat overstated his case in order to grab O'Connor's attention. In truth he did, in fact, have some options available in Trinidad and Tobago; however, the scared teenage version of Teague was determined to come to NIU and study with O'Connor and Alexis. Although the cornfields of Illinois are far removed from the steelpan mecca of Trinidad and Tobago, they are also a long way from the rough neighborhoods of Teague's youth, and the teenage pannist saw NIU as his musical oasis for better or worse.

Emotionally touched by the letter and remembering Teague's extraordinary musical gifts, O'Connor set about facilitating his admittance to NIU. Making Teague's dream of attending NIU a reality proved more problematic than O'Connor and Alexis initially suspected, and the entire process took nearly two years. First, despite his plea for help and his demonstrated virtuosic skills on steelpan, Teague, though a bright young man, had an underwhelming academic record in secondary school and was initially rejected from admission to NIU. To complicate matters further, Teague had some formal musical training and was proficient in note reading and music theory, but because of the differences in the requirements of American versus Trinidadian universities, he was deficient in some general academic areas. O'Connor pressed Teague's case, though, and ultimately convinced the university admissions counselors to admit the pannist based purely on Teague's promise and demonstrated work ethic.

With Teague admitted to NIU, O'Connor and Alexis then set about the task of paying for his education. According to NIU admission standards of the early 1990s, non-Illinois resident and international students were required to pay tuition three times that of in-state students. As such, O'Connor would need to secure enough scholarship funds to cover the cost of a large tuition waiver, as Teague and his family had little resources to cover the monumental costs. Through his local connections in DeKalb, O'Connor was able to secure enough funding from a local anonymous benefactor to cover tuition completely for the first year, two-thirds for the second year, and one-third each for years three and four of the baccalaureate degree. Joy Caesar, then Vice President of Citibank Trinidad and Tobago, who was also the director of the Southernaires Choir in San Fernando, helped arrange a partial scholarship for Teague. Through the help of Citibank Trinidad and Tobago, several benefit concerts, and various other organizations in Trinidad and Tobago, Teague raised enough funds to cover living expenses for his first year of study.[23] O'Connor was insistent: "I told him, I don't know how we're going to work this out, but come!"[24]

Teague enrolled the following academic semester for the spring of 1993 at NIU in the undergraduate steelpan degree program and set about his studies. O'Connor and Alexis set about finding more funds to pay Teague's living expenses and the remainder of his tuition. The NIU Steelband began immediately using him as a guest soloist to play with the band at various concerts at the University of Kentucky, Miami University of Ohio, and others. According to O'Connor, "We charged a $1000 each time he played," and the money went directly to Teague to pay his school expenses.[25] The additional income was welcome; however, Teague was limited to only a few of these paid engagements by the restrictions of his student visa. Because of the out-of-state tuition and his living costs, by the middle of his second year at NIU (1994–1995) funding was proving elusive. Without the emergence of a new funding source, it was looking more and more as if Teague would have to return to Trinidad without finishing his studies.

Serendipity has a great sense of timing, and for O'Connor, Alexis, Teague, and the NIU steelband program serendipity came in the form of Lester Trilla. When Alexis first came to NIU in 1985, he searched the Chicago metro for a suitable distributor of raw 55-gallon oil drums from which to make steelpans. Initially, Alexis purchased his raw oil drums from the Van Leer Container Corporation, which had a manufacturing plant in Alsip, Illinois. The Van Leer Container Corporation was familiar to Alexis as at the time they supplied many steelbands in Trinidad with oil barrels for making steelpans.[26] For the first few years at NIU, Alexis used barrels from Van Leer, but over time he became displeased with the quality of the drums and began searching for another distributor. Alexis heard about a place on the south side of Chicago called Trilla Steel Drum Manufacturing and, finding the barrel quality to his liking, began buying drums from the company. The quality of the barrels was excellent and, importantly, very consistent. Alexis became a regular at Trilla Steel Drum Manufacturing. As O'Connor recalls, "It got to the point where he [Alexis] would just pull his van up to the front of the place, the guys would load the barrels in for him, he'd pay and leave, no [purchase order], no nothing!"[27]

Word of "steelpan guy Cliff" made its way around the Trilla Steel Drum Manufacturing, all the way to the company president, Lester Trilla. Trilla Steel Drum Manufacturing and Lester Trilla were no strangers to steelpan, as Trilla's father had previously supplied oil barrels to the US Navy Steel Band in order to make steelpans in the 1950s and 1960s. Finally, during one of Alexis's routine trips to pick up oil drums, he and Trilla were introduced. Trilla is a naturally curious person and quizzed Alexis on all matters surrounding steelpans, steelpan building, and steelpan tuning. Once he found out that Alexis was also an educator from NIU, Trilla donated the drums, saying, "When he told me what the drums were for, I made my people give him the money back because, at the time, he was buying drums. I said we'll donate the drums. It's not a big problem."[28]

Trilla was charmed by Alexis and impressed with his knowledge of steel, and the two men hit it off. Trilla asked Alexis to perform solo steelpan at a party he was having with local businessmen a few weeks later. As Alexis recalls, "He [Trilla] told me to meet him at the factory and we'd drive together. I was waiting at the factory for him and all of the sudden, he pulls up, in a red Ferrari! Top down! I loaded my pans and away we go, down Michigan Avenue with my pans sticking out the back!"[29] From this point onward, the two made it a point to connect whenever Alexis came to the factory to buy drums. Alexis urged Trilla

FIGURE 8.1. Liam Teague and Lester Trilla at the Trilla Steel Drum Factory (late 1990s)

to come to NIU for a spring concert. "I kept telling him, you got to come down and see the band!"[30] Trilla finally relented and said that for the next concert (Spring 1994) he would try to attend. He was going to be flying back from business in Italy the day before, but he would hopefully make the drive down to DeKalb. Trilla made the trip to DeKalb, and what he saw and heard changed his life. "I opened up the doors and saw the lights, the red drums, and the kids playing up there, standing room only back then, it was just unbelievable."[31] Trilla later added, "I stood over there [pointing to stage left]. I just could not believe it, all these young people playing steelpan. It was fantastic! I just couldn't believe it!"[32]

After the concert, he sought out O'Connor and Alexis to congratulate the pair. But for Trilla, a heartfelt pat on the back was not all he had in mind. He was in a strong position financially and decided right then and there to be the NIU Steelband's benefactor. Trilla promptly said to O'Connor and Alexis, "How can I help?" and the pair responded, "You see this guy over here [Teague], he needs help paying for school or else he'll have to go back to Trinidad."[33] Trilla replied, "Done," and in only a few short weeks all of the arrangements were made. Trilla funded a scholarship to cover the final two years of Teague's undergraduate education.

The match between Trilla and NIU was a perfect fit, and he quickly became an integral part of the NIU Steelband family. Trilla attends as many concerts as he can and is a common sight around the steelband rehearsal space at NIU. Trilla was excited about the NIU Steelband and made it his mission to support the band. According to Trilla, "It's my social part of life. I don't play golf, I don't do a lot of things other people do."[34] Some patrons of the arts are often distant from the actual artists, a faceless name; however, Trilla is of a different sort and treats the NIU Steelband and the students he supports on scholarship as extended family. NIU Steelband alumnus Obe Quarless noted that Trilla "spends as much time as he can getting to know the students, meeting the new faces, finding out who's who."[35] Trilla often establishes lasting relationships with the students of the NIU Steelband, and alumnus Kenneth Joseph regularly emails Trilla and updates him on his continuing work as a pannist. Like other NIU Steelband alumni, Joseph continues to let Trilla know how much his aid was, and still is, appreciated.[36]

Trilla and his company have since helped more than a dozen students earn degrees in steelpan performance through his generous scholarship and graduate assistantship support. The establishment of the graduate assistantship position for the NIU Steelband is a win/win situation as it allows the students to work at NIU and earn experience while also better handling the financial peculiarities of international students attending the university. The Trilla graduate assistantship, however, was not yet established in 1997, when Teague was seeking admission to NIU, and after he graduated from NIU with an undergraduate degree in music, Teague's future was still in question. Fate was once again on Teague's side, and the Enron Corporation, which had major energy holdings in Trinidad and Tobago, stepped in to help. The company had previously paid a portion of Teague's undergraduate education; upon hearing of his predicament, it offered to pay the entirety of his graduate degree tuition at NIU. According to Enron Managing Director Ed Freedburg, "Your [Teague's] inevitable contribution to the steelband movement, the culture and the people of Trinidad and Tobago will be very gratifying to us."[37] With the continued support of Enron, Teague immediately enrolled in the master of music in percussion performance program with a steelpan emphasis at NIU, and earned his degree in 1997.

CHAPTER 9

RETURN TO TRINIDAD AND THE WORLD STEELBAND MUSIC FESTIVAL 2000

> It's not just a school we operate at NIU, it's a brotherhood. It means a lot for us to play in this World Festival. It is an experience. The instrument is being played by Universities around the world. We don't think about coming to compete and win. There is no axe to grind. It's all about the experience. I have always talked to my students about pan in Trinidad and Tobago. Now they can witness all that I told them first hand.
>
> —Cliff Alexis (2000)[1]

From the time Alexis joined O'Connor at NIU in 1985, the pair shared a hope that some day they would be able to bring the NIU Steelband to Trinidad. Beyond showing off the progress of steelpan in the United States, O'Connor and Alexis wanted to expose NIU students to the real flesh and blood of steelpan's roots. In October of 2000, the NIU Steelband finally got its chance to sojourn to the birthplace of steelpan as participants in the World Steelband Music Festival (hereafter WSMF) competition. The WSMF was an outgrowth of the biannual nationwide steelband competition Pan Is Beautiful. For the 2000 installment of Pan Is Beautiful, a decision was made by officials of Pan Trinbago to invite steelbands from outside Trinidad and Tobago to participate, and it therefore temporarily changed the festival name to the World Steelband Music Festival.

The Pan Is Beautiful steelband festival has a long history, having originated in Trinidad and Tobago in 1952. Colonial Trinidad (pre-1962) held music festivals and competitions for conventional European instruments as early as 1948, if not earlier, and, inspired by the rousing success of TASPO's (Trinidad All-Steel Percussion Orchestra) trip to Europe in

1950,[2] a special category for steelbands was created. For the first competition in 1952, classical music was optional, and the test piece was an arrangement of a popular calypso-style tune. The inclusion of steelpan was a success, and British judge Dr. Sydney Northcote commented, "We have witnessed man's ingenuity in trying to get beauty out of something that is absolutely a waste product."[3] Over the years, regular festivals with steelband competitions continued and became a biannual institution. After a brief hiatus during the 1970s, the festivals were restarted in the 1980s under the name Pan Is Beautiful; as part of this revived tradition, the National Schools steelband competition was added as a separate element in 1981.

For the World Steelband Music Festival in 2000, Pan Trinbago's decision to invite steelbands from around the globe posed several substantial logistical problems, the most pressing of which was narrowing down the number of participants. Festival organizers set a semifinal roster with sixteen slots available; six of these were reserved for foreign bands. In 1998, Pan Is Beautiful served double duty as the island-wide steelband competition and as the preliminary qualifying round for the WSMF for Trinidad and Tobago steelbands. Steelbands from across the country were invited to participate.[4] For Pan Is Beautiful in 1998, O'Connor was again invited back to Trinidad and Tobago as one of the foreign judges. Shortly after his return to DeKalb from Trinidad, two Pan Trinbago officials, Richard Forteau and Junia Regrello, came to NIU on a fact-finding mission. The pair announced to O'Connor and Alexis that Pan Trinbago was planning the World Steelband Music Festival, and impressed by the steelband program at NIU, they invited the NIU Steelband to compete.[5]

The presence of Pan Trinbago officials at NIU inspired Alexis and O'Connor to think about the possibilities of taking a group of students and alumni to Trinidad to compete in the WSMF. Many logistical issues had to be worked out to even consider such a trip for the NIU Steelband, and atop the list was money. Alexis recalled, "In the back of my head, I wondered if the event would come off and if we were going to enter."[6] After serious deliberation O'Connor and Alexis decided to accept the invitation, and the NIU Steelband was set to head to Trinidad and Tobago.

Three European steelbands were also chosen through a preliminary competition held in Paris, France at the Parc de la Villette in May of 2000. There was, however, no preliminary competition staged in the United States. In addition to NIU, steelbands from New York (CASYM) and Florida (Florida Memorial University) were invited to participate. In all, the WSMF competition hosted steel orchestras (large steelbands), ensembles (single steelpan steelbands), and soloists from England, France, Switzerland, Finland, the United States, Grenada, Jamaica, St. Lucia, and Trinidad and Tobago. The judges for the WSMF competition were Dr. Anne Osborne (Trinidad and Tobago), Richard Murphy (England), and Dr. Eugene Novotney (USA).

Once the decision was made to attend the WSMF, O'Connor immediately began tackling the logistics, letter writing, planning, and other administrative details necessary to ensure that NIU had a full-sounding steelband for the festival. As a result of O'Connor and Alexis's request, Pan Trinbago indicated that the festival would be held in June of 2000 in order to accommodate the academic calendar of NIU and take advantage of cheaper out-of-season airfare to Trinidad and Tobago for the American steelbands. However, during the late stages of planning, Pan Trinbago reversed course, and the festival dates were moved to September and then October of that same year to instead better accommodate the European steelbands. For the American steelbands, NIU in particular, this created a major problem, as the new festival dates landed in the middle of the fall semester. For the NIU Steelband, a new semester meant new players, and these new players faced a steep learning curve. According to O'Connor, "We were trying to keep some of our graduates to represent NIU but when the dates were changed the graduates moved on and we had to train new people; six of them to be exact in sections such as the quadrophonics, a drummer, a bass, and three tenors."[7] In order to fill out the sections with strong players, O'Connor and Alexis called on several NIU alumni living in Trinidad and Tobago. These included Harold Headley, the first Trinidadian to attain a master's degree in music with a concentration in steelpan, Denise Lowe, Satanand Sharma, Elizabeth Flocker-Aming, and Liam Teague.

While Alexis focused on making steelpans and arranging the NIU Steelband's competition tunes, O'Connor took on organizing the fundraising. O'Connor estimated the total cost of the trip would be around $30,000; however the final cost was much more.[8] A major portion of the funds for the trip were donated by the NIU Foundation, and other supplemental funds came via smaller donations from individual sources, CD sales, and proceeds from NIU steelband performances.[9] Pan Trinbago paid the hotel and ground transportation expenses of the foreign bands.[10] However, funding for other incidental expenses was left undefined, and the total cost submitted to NIU was merely an estimate—a cause of great consternation for O'Connor and Alexis. Pan Trinbago was also evasive regarding the total cost to participate and appeared unsure about what their own costs for hosting the event would total. Patrick Arnold, president of Pan Trinbago, told the *Trinidad Newsday*, "Take for example we have Northern Illinois University Steelband arriving the day before their scheduled performance. So only after the participants get here will we actually know the overall cost to host them."[11] One such cost for foreign steelbands was securing rehearsal space in Trinidad, and another was arranging for the use of instruments. Shipping their own steelpans from DeKalb to Trinidad would be a costly endeavor, likely prohibitively so.

Further, considering the non-standardization of steelpan construction in Trinidad and Tobago, ensuring that NIU students would have instruments in Trinidad that were consistent with those in DeKalb was a major concern. O'Connor estimated that he would need to ship or carry on the airplane seventy cases of steelpans. Pan Trinbago initially had promised foreign steelbands a discount on freight to ship instruments; however, when the promise fell through O'Connor pleaded with BWIA and Amerijet International Air Freight for a discount in freight in exchange for sponsorship of the NIU Steelband and prime billing in the concert program.[12] With skyrocketing transportation costs threatening to derail their plans, O'Connor and Alexis proposed an alternate solution in which they would bring the frontline steelpans on the plane as checked baggage and Alexis would fly down to Trinidad ahead of the NIU Steelband and make the bass steelpans. Alexis later told the *Trinidad Newsday*, "We were promised a discount of 20 percent on airfare from Chicago to Trinidad for the Festival and 50 percent on freight. ... Being a native of Trinidad, I suggested to the University the idea of me coming home [to Trinidad] ahead of time and making the background (bass) pans significantly reducing our overheads."[13] Alexis was able to negotiate with Pan Trinbago to utilize their steelpan factory site in El Soccorro, and he arrived in Trinidad ten days ahead of the NIU Steelband. Like the trip to Taiwan, Alexis worked twelve-hour days for nine days in order to get the instruments ready for NIU players, but upon the band's arrival in Trinidad, the steelpans were ready.

The NIU Steelband arrived in Trinidad on the last day of the competition's semifinals round and, with little time to spare, rehearsed and then performed. Their strategy of building and securing their own instruments proved to be an important competitive strategy for the band. The time saved by not having to acclimate to new instruments (possibly with different note layouts) gave the players more time to concentrate on drilling the music. Many other foreign bands participating in the WSMF, however, were not so lucky and had to borrow instruments from Trinidadian steelbands and relearn note patterns in a limited amount of time. Jenny Lee, vice president of Steelpan European at the time and the coordinator of the participating European steelbands, told the *Trinidad Guardian*, "[The European steelbands] had to borrow instruments from various steelbands, including Witco Desperadoes, BP Renegades and Pamberi."[14] The competitive disadvantage notwithstanding, Lee later suggested that borrowing steelpans from Trinidadian steelbands was a positive aspect of cultural exchange. "If Calypsociation [the French band who participated] didn't have to borrow pans, they would have never come into contact with the people from the local bands."[15]

With the logistical issue of steelpans resolved, O'Connor and Alexis turned their attention to securing a proper rehearsal space for the NIU Steelband in Trinidad. Several foreign steelbands rehearsed on the grounds or parking lots of their respective hotels, which presented complications for all involved. For example, Calypsociation rehearsed in the courtyard of the Cascadia Hotel, much to the chagrin of other hotel guests, who were far from enamored with the constant ringing of steelpans into the late hours of the night. When guests started complaining to management and throwing tumblers of water onto the band from the balcony above, hotel management informed Calypsociation that they would no longer be able to rehearse after 9:00 pm. The situation was lambasted in the *Trinidad Guardian*: "Under the scorching heat of the noonday sun members of French Steelband, Calypsociation, rehearsed their classical piece."[16] The NIU Steelband, however, fared significantly better as Alexis called in favors to his good friend Len "Boogsie" Sharpe and secured the panyard of the Phase II steelband as the temporary home of the NIU Steelband.

With the logistical issues of the instruments, rehearsal space, and hotel accommodations set, the choice of competition pieces was a central focus. The band had to perform three arrangements including a tune of choice, a calypso, and a test piece. For the tune of choice and the calypso, the NIU Steelband chose two original compositions. For the tune of choice, they chose Robert Chappell's "Wood-n-Steel," and for the calypso, they chose a new arrangement called "Pan 2000," composed by Cliff Alexis specifically for the festival.

FIGURE 9.1. World Steelband Music Festival Competition performance (2000)

"Wood-n-Steel" was the NIU Steelband's secret weapon. As discussed earlier, Robert Chappell had composed "Wood-n-Steel" in 1991 for the NIU Steelband's first tour to Taiwan in March 1992. Despite being nearly a decade old, the arrangement was unknown in Trinidad and Tobago. O'Connor and Alexis were sure that, with its unique sound and thrilling Amadinda xylophone cadenza, "Wood-n-Steel" would be a bona fide showstopper. The work was not like anything else in the steelband canon, and it really showcased the range of the NIU Steelband musicians. Yet, concerned about the fickle nature of steelband judging in Trinidad and Tobago, O'Connor and Alexis triple-checked competition rules regarding the use of extraneous percussion instruments before selecting "Wood-n-Steel" as their tune of choice.[17]

The test piece required of every steelband competing in the WSMF was source for much consternation for all participants in the competition. The piece was composed by Rudolph F. Wells and entitled "Dawn of the Millennium." The piece was very problematic and fraught with compositional peculiarities and part-copying errors. Given that the NIU Steelband was under severe time restrictions in learning the three compositions for the WSMF, O'Connor and Alexis made a calculated decision to spend as little time and effort as possible in preparing and drilling the test piece. Seeking clarity on the issues plaguing "Dawn of the Millennium," O'Connor reached out to Pan Trinbago officials, who eventually sent the NIU Steelband a list of no fewer than thirty-nine errata queries.[18] O'Connor and Alexis's hedge had paid off, and problems with the composition led organizers of the WSMF to drop the piece as a requirement for the competition's final round. In addition, having each competing steelband perform three arrangements made the program dreadfully long, and the decision to drop "Dawn of the Millennium" from the final-round requirements was further justified as a logistical time-saving measure.[19]

Tragically, steelbands such as the Caribbean Airlines Invaders Steel Orchestra spent considerable amounts of effort learning incorrect versions of "Dawn of the Millennium" given to them by Pan Trinbago only to receive comments from the judges such as, "Which version were you playing?"[20] In Pan Is Beautiful competitions from years past, ignoring the details of the test piece could mean the difference between a steelband's finishing in first or fifth place. *Trinidad Guardian* columnist Peter Ray Blood captured the overall feeling of the test piece with his new titling "Yawn of the Millennium."[21] Keith Smith of the *Trinidad Express* echoed these sentiments, commenting, "I was happy to be spared the humbug of a test piece played yawningly over and over."[22]

The WSMF formally opened on October 12, 2000, at the Jean Pierre Complex with a parade of nations; the program also introduced the adjudicators, and festival chairman Patrick Arnold gave welcoming remarks. The national anthem for each participating country was performed by a representative of each foreign steelband. The NIU Steelband's Paul G. Ross performed the United States' national anthem on tenor steelpan. Caught unaware of the ritual at such festivals, none of the American steelbands (NIU, CASYM, or Florida Memorial) had thought to bring an American flag, and one was borrowed for the occasion from the US embassy in Trinidad and Tobago.

The NIU Steelband performed admirably in the semifinal round and earned a spot in the final round the following weekend. Their performance was labeled a "crowd pleaser" in local newspapers as the band displayed its skills on steelpan. Furthermore, the NIU Steelband received special praise for its acknowledgment of the African roots of steelband as depicted in the tune of choice "Wood-n-Steel." The final round of the WSMF was held the following Saturday night, October 21, when the eight finalists—evenly split with four foreign and four domestic bands—vied for the title of world champion. The NIU Steelband led off the competition, not an easy spot for any steelband to perform, and the band donned red NIU Steelband t-shirts and black pants, representing their school colors with pride.

As the last steelband performed and the results were tabulated, the performers anxiously waited for the announcement of their fate. According to co-author Remy, "I was standing close to Al [O'Connor] when they were about to announce the placement in backwards order. I distinctly remember him saying, "Did they call NIU? They called NIU? We took second?!"[23] O'Connor's disbelief was quickly overtaken by the screams of joy from NIU Steelband members, who were in a state of euphoria. The steelband from America had risen in the rankings from eight in the semifinals to second overall and they had nearly won the whole competition—an amazing feat indeed.

For the students and staff of the NIU Steelband, performing in the WSMF was not about winning as much as it was about representing the future of steelpan and the reach of steelpan as of the end of the millennium. According to O'Connor, "What we've done still hasn't sunk in, it was just an amazing experience. The students will never forget this for the rest of their lives. The reputation of this group has grown worldwide now. There's no question about it!"[24] Taking second place at the WSMF was a triumph, no doubt, and during the bedlam of the results announcements that followed, members of the NIU Steelband rushed the stage and proudly carried away stage accoutrements (posters and banners) as souvenirs (some are still displayed in the steelband room at NIU to this day). When the NIU Steelband arrived back in DeKalb two days later, the band was given a hero's welcome. A proud chair of the NIU School of Music, Paul Bauer, proclaimed, "NIU really pulled out all the stops for the finals, simply amazing!"[25] The NIU Steelband was now internationally recognized as one of the best steelbands in the world, a very proud moment for the history of the NIU Steelband, the university, the School of Music, NIU Steelband members, faculty, and staff.

After the conclusion of the WSMF festival, the prize money was distributed. For their stunning second-place finish the NIU Steelband won $18,000 USD, a windfall that O'Connor and Alexis were not expecting.[26] When the prize money arrived at DeKalb the following month, O'Connor and Alexis graciously gave a portion back to the managers of the Phase II Steel Orchestra. "There was never an expectation we would break even. When the prize money came, we paid a portion of it to Phase II as rental fee for the use of their panyard, although they never asked for anything."[27] The instruments that Alexis had made in Trinidad were donated to several local Trinidadian secondary schools as an offering of good faith. One such recipient was Hillview College (Trinidadian high schools are often referred to as "colleges"), the alma mater of Satanand Sharma—current lecturer in music at UWI–St. Augustine and an NIU Steelband alumnus.

The WSMF 2000 was eye-opening for many Trinidadians who were unaware or dismissive of just how far the steelpan had developed in the United States, Canada, Europe, and the greater Caribbean in recent decades. For many Trinidadians, it was shocking and surprising to witness the dedication and aptitude that foreigners displayed in grasping the art of steelband. Peter Blood, a concerned *Trinidad Guardian* columnist, surmised that "one just has to observe the attitude, commitment and dedication, panmanship of the musicians that comprise visiting bands such as Pan Lovers, Northern Illinois University, CASYM, as well as that of the Japanese and Germans to appreciate just how precarious our position is."[28] For other Trinidadians, the gains made by foreign bands were a de facto call to action. Well-known Trinidadian steelpan figure Pat Bishop spoke in terms not yet heard in Trinidad and Tobago, stating that there was a "competitive disadvantage" of the Trinidadian steelbands in comparison to the NIU Steelband, whose members could read sheet music. Len "Boogsie" Sharpe, victoriously leading the Trinidadian band Skiffle Bunch to the title, told the *Trinidad Express*, "I hope that the people who have to deal with pan and pannists now understand the work that we have been doing all the years, which is how these bands from those other countries have been able to come here and put on such a show. The whole festival brought a shake-up in the pan world and, in fact, I would say in the country."[29]

For his part, O'Connor was more pointed about what the NIU Steelband's near win meant in the greater scheme of the competition, noting, "We've changed the whole way they're going to have to look at the pieces they're going to have to play in the future. It's time to stop following the same format where they adapt a previously composed classical piece."[30] Case in point was the overwhelming success of the piece "Wood-n-Steel," which wowed audiences in each round of the competition and was the crowd-pleasing talk of the Trinidadian steelpan community following the WSMF.[31] According to O'Connor, "Our

"Wood-n-Steel" piece just blew everyone away. We won the 'tune of choice' category in every single level of the event. I talked with the English judge [Richard Murphy] at length at the reception. He was just astounded. I talked to reporters from Europe and Jamaica. The kind of stuff we presented was so unusual, so different."[32]

NIU School of Music Chair Paul Bauer's summary of the NIU Steelband's achievement at the WSMF put an exclamation point on the accomplishment. "This event is important historically in that never before has a foreign band ever gotten to the finals of the World Steelband Music Festival, never before has a foreign band been a challenge to a Trinidad/Tobago band and 'Wood-n-Steel' and 'Pan 2000' were considered innovations to this competition."[33]

CHAPTER 10

STEELPAN DEGREE PROGRAM AND THE NIU/UWI PIPELINE

> In light of the initiatives taken by Northern Illinois University, it seems quite sad that we have not yet set up a school of music for our pannists. Why was our own Anthony Prospect not given the support for such a project? If the steelband movement is to take an international leap, if qualified pannists are to establish our music in various parts of the world, will they come from TT or Northern Illinois? Or will we be sending our steelbandsmen to Northern Illinois on scholarship to acquire degrees in pan music?
>
> —*Trinidad Guardian*, November 25, 1989[1]

One of the most important factors spurring Alexis to join O'Connor in DeKalb in 1985 was the hope that someday NIU might establish a free-standing degree program in steelpan. O'Connor, too, shared this vision, and the pair worked steadily over the course of several years to divorce steelpan from the overarching umbrella of the percussion department and to create a curriculum that put the steelpan on equal footing with the violin, piano, or voice in the NIU School of Music. According to O'Connor, "It was my intention from the beginning to think of steel drums not as a novelty, but to have people learn the music of where they came from."[2] Alexis in particular, was adamant that NIU admit as many qualified Trinidadian, Caribbean, and other foreign-born students as possible to study in the steelband program. He knew firsthand the struggles, and subsequent waste, of many a talented Trinidadian pannist who gave up pursuing steelpan as a vocation because of a lack of opportunity in Trinidad and Tobago. Approaching his task head on, Alexis told the *Trinidad Guardian*, "With work like this, you can't sit in one place too long. There's a message to be spoken and you have to use lots of different platforms."³

Though the progression accelerated with the arrival of Alexis in 1985, the process of creating a university degree in steelpan began way back during the mid-1970s. In the latter part of the 1970s, O'Connor became convinced that steelband was a viable economic avenue for NIU percussion graduates to pursue and that the instrument should be a core component of any bachelor's or master's degree in percussion. However, O'Connor, and later Alexis, would need to convince the NIU administration of the necessity of a degree in steelpan in order for them to fully accept the instrument as a legitimate instrument of study in academia.

In general, the NIU administration and faculty were supportive of the idea, though O'Connor recalls that they were not without their detractors.

> We had a ... professor on our music education faculty, who was kind of like a crotchety old [guy].... They used to have this event here ... called Spring Fest, [which was] a week-long festival, and the student association would usually hire us to open it up, and we would play out on the student center.... And he would just keep going on and on about what a bunch of nonsense this [steelband music] all was, and I said, "Well look, why don't [you] come over and hear it sometime and then maybe you could make a decision." And so I invited him to the opening program and I happened to see him kind of hiding in the back of the audience and everything. And as was always the case, we had a huge crowd there to hear us and they all loved it. So we brought the instruments back to the building here and I ran into him later in the afternoon, and I said, "Frank, what did you think?" And he said, "You know what I don't like about that steelband? There isn't anybody that doesn't like it."⁴

O'Connor was very pragmatic in creating the necessary conditions for convincing the NIU administration of the importance and necessity for a degree in steelpan. In defense of steelband, he surmised that not only does it offer opportunities for music major ensemble participation, it excels at drawing non–music majors and non-musicians from the college or university general student body to come and participate.

O'Connor created an atmosphere in the NIU percussion department during the late 1970s in which students such as James Campbell and Jeff Bush were free to explore the steelpan and focus extra effort on the instrument. Beginning in 1981, steelband was added as an ensemble to the course catalog at NIU as a stand-alone course for credit, the first of its kind in the world. In 1983, Trinidadian Leonard Moses became the first person to earn a degree in percussion from NIU in which he focused almost exclusively on steelpan as his primary percussion instrument. In the mid-1980s several students (Jeannine Remy, for example) earned bachelor's and master's degrees in percussion in which they focused heavily on steelpan. Others such as Sarah Barnes-Tsai created individualized master's degrees in world music with the aid of O'Connor and NIU ethnomusicologist professor Han. In 1986, Paulette Frazier and Twyla Cole followed Alexis from St. Paul, Minnesota, and were the first undergraduate steelpan majors at NIU.⁵

Acclimating the NIU administration to the value of steelband took decades; yet, by the fall of 1989, the NIU School of Music was comfortable enough with steelpan to allow a master's degree in music performance with a steelpan emphasis. In 1991, history was made when Harold Headley became the first person to graduate from an American university with a graduate degree in music with an emphasis in steelpan. Headley arrived at NIU quite by accident, having honed his musicianship skills as a young adult with Louise McIntosh and her famed Pan Pipers Music School of St. Augustine, Trinidad. Later, he toured the United States with the Trinidad Tripoli Steelband in the late 1960s and early 1970s. McIntosh told Headley that he had "too much talent to waste" and pushed him to consider pursuing an education in the United States. As Headley recalled, "I applied to many schools and said to myself, 'I am going to attend the first university to accept me as a student.'" As fate would have it, the first university to accept Headley was the University of Wisconsin–Oshkosh where Trinidadian Sean Lewis, also a former student of McIntosh, was finishing a music degree. The University of Wisconsin–Oshkosh was not exactly a musical mecca in the 1980s, and the university had only a small music department and no steelband of any sort. Headley studied classical and jazz percussion and, in a formal academy setting, diligently focused on the basics of harmony, theory, ear training, and music history required of traditional music students at the University of Wisconsin–Oshkosh.

When Alexis got wind that Headley was in Oshkosh (some 180 miles from DeKalb), he immediately invited him to NIU as a guest artist in 1987. Headley and Alexis had been acquaintances since 1967 when, as Headley explained, "We were both performing at Expo '67 [in Montreal] together but in separate bands. He was in the National Steelband and I was in Tripoli."[6] His guest performance with the NIU Steelband was a success, and Headley, greatly impressed with the program that O'Connor and Alexis had in place, sought counsel from the NIU panmen regarding his future prospects. If one were to teach at the college level in the United States, a graduate degree was necessary, and Headley began plotting his future course of study.

After graduating from the University of Wisconsin–Oshkosh, Headley took a year off and went back to Trinidad. Once back home, Headley noticed, "NIU was the school everyone was talking about when it came to anything that had to do with steelpan or steelband."[7] The decision was easy, and Headley returned to NIU, this time in pursuit of his master's degree. O'Connor and Alexis arranged for a scholarship audition, and Headley was awarded a substantial scholarship. Because international students pay higher tuition, Headley remembered that the scholarship was barely "enough to pay tuition and room and board. . . . While I was at NIU, I was working with the steelband and giving arranging lessons to a few of the students."[8]

As a true pannist, in contrast to a percussionist who plays steelpan, Headley's arrival required O'Connor and Alexis to devise a steelpan major degree using the existing degree framework available at NIU. Headley recalls, "Al was still the chairman, or something like that, so he could pull a few strings." O'Connor devised a music curriculum specifically for the needs of a steelpan major at the graduate level and packaged the degree as an "individual" major. The primary focus of Headley's degree plan was jazz improvisation (with steelpan as his primary instrument) and composition. Jazz combo was the small ensemble of choice, and steelband served as the large ensemble.[9] His degree plan was combined years later with another version created by Professor Han for an individualized major in world music to become the model degree plan for steelpan graduate degree candidates at NIU.

The needs of the Trinidadian pannists, Headley included, were much different from those of American students trained in the standard academic setting. According to O'Connor, Trinidadian steelpan students typically have tremendous musical ears and memorize music quickly—all this, of course, is a direct result of the Panorama and education tradition in Trinidad and Tobago, which features rote learning and endless repetition, rather than a grounding in musical notation, sight reading, and scores. According to NIU alumnus and Trinidadian Seion Gomez, "Well, as you know, Trinidadians have a real good sense of hearing music and memorizing it after one time. What NIU taught me was the best of both worlds: reading and listening."[10] O'Connor quickly learned that many Trinidadian students, even the most accomplished of musicians, are grossly deficient in sight reading and sometimes require explanations of fundamental harmony concepts known only to them via their musical ears. Headley recalls, "Al took me under his wing and he even practiced sight-reading with me."[11] Regardless, steelpan majors were treated like any other major at NIU, and this meant a full spectrum of juries, studio class performances, and recitals. In 1991 Harold Headley became the first NIU music major to complete a master's degree with an emphasis in steelpan as a major instrument.

Despite the success of Moses and Headley, the boundaries that existed because of the institutional requirements of the NIU School of Music prevented a more regular influx of Trinidadian students from attending NIU. Furthermore, O'Connor and Alexis faced serious hurdles in facilitating and accepting students from Trinidad and Tobago for study at NIU. First and foremost, the NIU School of Music was subject to the National Association of Schools of Music admission standards, which required completed bachelor's degrees for master's degree studies. Whereas O'Connor and Alexis saw, and continue to see, the establishment of a steelpan degree at NIU as a valuable resource to pannists the world over, in Trinidad and Tobago there was distress that it was an American university that was the first to take these steps. The *Trinidad Guardian* lamented this reality, stating, "The news that Northern Illinois University in the United States is offering a bachelor of arts degree in steelband music should make us ashamed of our failure to date to do so ourselves at our own University of the West Indies."[12]

The exclusion of steelband from Trinidadian university curricula was, in many ways, a lasting vestige of the Trinidadian steelband movement's struggles during the 1950s and 1960s—a time of bad johns and gang warfare among the various steelbands. Others in Trinidad used NIU's achievement of a steelpan degree program as a call to action, and the opinion sections of Trinidadian newspapers, with their long and storied history of pointed social criticism, praised the achievement of O'Connor and Alexis: "All praise to Northern Illinois University and Professor Allan O'Connor and Trinidadian Cliff Alexis who are actually running the course. . . . It seems quite sad that we have not yet set up a School of Music for our pannists."[13]

FIGURE 10.1. Liam Teague as Graduate Student Concertizing in Taiwan (late 1990s)

Finally in 1992, nearly twenty years after NIU began using steelband as an element of the percussion ensemble (1973) and eleven years after the university made steelband an accredited course (1981), the University of the West Indies–St. Augustine, Trinidad (hereafter UWI–St. Augustine) began to offer courses in steelpan—the country's national instrument. Momentum for the inclusion of steelband in Trinidadian universities began building in 1990, when Clive Pantin, then Trinidad and Tobago's education minister, announced that a school of music would be established at UWI–St. Augustine. Officials in Pan Trinbago, the Trinidadian Government Departments of Culture and Education, and the United Nations Educational, Scientific and Cultural Organization (UNESCO) assisted in writing a curriculum that was presented and passed by the UWI–St. Augustine faculty board in the late spring of 1992.[14]

The first music certificate classes began in the fall of 1992 with steelpan as a special component. Upon the final approval in late 1992 by the UWI–St. Augustine faculty board, music classes and a steelpan degree program began in the second semester of 1993. Five years later, in 1997, UWI–St. Augustine began offering a bachelor of arts with steelpan as the primary instrument of study. According to the music department chair, Dr. Osborne, one of the major goals of offering the new steelpan degree was "to promote music literacy in Trinidad and Tobago."[15] With the bachelor of arts degree in place, the UWI–St. Augustine steelpan program quickly established a close relationship with NIU and started serving as a feeder institution for prospective students attending NIU. Many of these students were fortunate enough to earn Lester Trilla scholarships, and still others received scholarships from various additional sources. The music students who received either certificates or bachelor's degrees from UWI–St. Augustine and continued onward to NIU to complete the graduate-degree program include Seion Gomez, BM 1999, MM 2007; Liz Flocker-Aming, MM 2001; Denise Lowe, MM 2001; Nadine Gonzales, MM 2003; Wayne Bruno, MM 2003; Gay Magnus, MM 2003; Sophia Subero, MM 2007; Kenneth Joseph, MM 2010; David Aarons, MM 2012; Barry Mannette, MM 2013; Khion de Las, MM 2013; Khan Cordice, MM 2015; and recent students Kareem "TJ" King and Akua Leith, MM 2016.

The benefits of the connection between NIU and UWI–St. Augustine have been substantial. The connection has provided a global perspective and served as an invaluable multicultural experience to American students in the program. According to Dean Rich Holly, the benefits of the connection flow both ways.

> Having the strong connection that we do with UWI enables students from Trinidad and Tobago to study in the United States with two of the most significant personalities in the world of steel pan, while providing an enriching cultural experience for the American students at NIU. It's a true win-win situation for all parties involved.[16]

Trinidadian alumni Satanand Sharma (MME 2002) sees the NIU-UWI connection as enriching for both institutions in the areas of music education and performance. "The NIU experiences add value to the UWI graduate and the UWI graduate enriches the steelpan program at NIU. There is lots of potential for further development in this relationship."[17]

In recent years, the success of the steelband program at UWI–St. Augustine and the University of Trinidad and Tobago has rekindled the debate about the validity of studying steelpan at NIU. According to Teague, "Many people there wonder, 'Why should we send our child to Northern Illinois University when they can receive a free education in Trinidad and Tobago?' But what we have to offer is so fantastic, and it complements what is available in Trinidad and Tobago."[18] Amazingly, nearly half of the current steelpan faculty at UWI–St. Augustine earned their degrees from NIU. This includes alumnus Harold Headley, who recently retired but is still teaching, Jeannine Remy, Satanand Sharma, Barry Mannette, and Khion de Las. With such a strong reciprocation of students and faculty, the connection between NIU and UWI–St. Augustine only stands to grow stronger in the coming years.

CHAPTER 11

O'CONNOR RETIRES, TEAGUE/ALEXIS ERA BEGINS

From its humble beginnings in 1973 through the high-profile tours and triumphs of the 1990s and early 2000s, Al O'Connor and Cliff Alexis were the identity of steelband at Northern Illinois University. After thirty-five years of teaching and service to NIU, O'Connor decided to fully retire in the summer of 2003, and protégé Liam Teague took over as co-director of the NIU Steelband. The announcement came as little surprise to those affiliated with the NIU steelband program as O'Connor had already retired from his position as associate dean of NIU's College of Visual and Performing Arts in the spring of 2000.[1] O'Connor continued on a phased-retirement plan as co-director of the NIU Steelband in part to usher Teague and Alexis through the transition and to aid the NIU Steelband's tours to Korea in 2002 for the World Cup festivities.

In a process that began prior to his graduation from NIU with a master's degree in steelpan in 1999, Teague was groomed to be O'Connor's successor as a steelband faculty member at NIU. Since his arrival on campus in the winter of 1993, Teague had been thrust to the fore by O'Connor and Alexis as a representative of the NIU steelband program in various capacities. Teague was constantly featured as a soloist with the NIU Steelband and as a guest artist with many other steelbands and traditional Western classical ensembles throughout the United States and the world. Countless awards and accolades followed the virtuoso, and there was no shortage of ink spilled by newspapers in Trinidad and Tobago and the United States chronicling his accomplishments.

Teague's journey was not, however, without its challenges. Despite the praise and adoration, by the fall of 1998, Teague was still in the same predicament as he had been in 1992 when he first contacted O'Connor and Alexis, pleading to come to NIU. Teague was set to finish his graduate degree in steelpan performance at NIU in the spring of 1999, and had, at the time, no solid plans for his future. Would he return to Trinidad? Would he try to extend his student visa and stay in the United States? Questions abounded, but the answers were few, and the reality of Teague's professional future was far from certain.

When talking about his dear friend and colleague Alexis, O'Connor conceded, "Cliff will probably never retire, he'll die with a hammer in his hand!"[2] For O'Connor, however, retirement was very much on his mind, and as the 1990s wore on, the end was in sight. He and Alexis talked on numerous occasions during the time that Teague was pursuing his master's degree about what should happen to Teague; that is, how to retain him at NIU and how to maintain the steelpan faculty tenure line within the NIU School of Music. O'Connor's faculty position, regardless of his actual duties with the NIU Steelband, was classified as "percussion professor generalist," which included classical percussion, drum set and the like—skills in which the pannist Teague was not trained. The matter also weighed on Dean Holly, too, and he contemplated possible ways in which Teague could be retained: "We knew we had to do something, anything, in order to keep him here."[3] Teague's ascent from student to professor at NIU was a process that evolved from his arrival on campus at NIU in January of 1993. His prodigious talent and reputation as a virtuoso pannist preceded him; however, it was Teague's vision for the future development of steelpan, and the steelband program at NIU, that greatly impressed O'Connor and Alexis.

Jan Bach's Concerto for Steelpan

From the day he arrived at NIU, Teague was interested in pushing himself and the boundaries of the steelpan. One way in which he did this was as a featured soloist with the NIU Steelband. When the NIU Steelband first went out on "run out" concerts after Liam arrived in 1993, he was used as a featured soloist, and audiences were shocked and mesmerized at his skill and technical proficiency. As Elizabeth DeLamater recalled, "I saw Liam overwhelmed by screaming high-school girls in Chicago one time. We were loading up the pans after the concert at a high school, and a girl saw him out the window and screamed there he is, and he just wasn't used to that. I just saw all of that. He was the sweetest guy. He just didn't know."[4]

Teague never envisioned himself becoming a teacher and often assumed that his role in steelpan would be as a featured soloist or recording artist, promoting the instrument throughout the globe. One particular performance, however, changed Teague's perception. In this sense Teague's premiere of Jan Bach's *Concerto for Steel Pan* with the Chicago Sinfonietta in November of 1995 was a transformative event. NIU composition professor Jan Bach was inspired to write a concerto for steelpan in the summer of 1994 after hearing Teague perform for the first time. In addition to his duties with the composition department at NIU, Bach is a celebrated American contemporary classical composer with a wide-ranging catalog that includes concertos, operas, string quartets, choral pieces, and dozens of other works for eclectic instrumentation. Bach was no stranger to the NIU Steelband and enjoyed hearing the band throughout his tenure at NIU. "I watched the development of the steelpan program at NIU from its inception and beginning by G. Allan O'Connor, the NIU percussion teacher and my fellow graduate student at the University of Illinois where we both played in the university orchestra."[5]

The NIU Steelband fascinated Bach, and he was especially impressed with their continued work performing classical music. "I was intrigued with the vitality of this medium and the fun our college students—mostly studying other degrees—obviously got out of playing in this ensemble, but I didn't take the group seriously until they reached the performance level to play transcriptions of traditional composers, including [J. S.] Bach chorales, which showed a level of sensitivity, dynamic contrast, and the performance skills necessary to play anything thrown at them."[6] While most steelbands in Trinidad and Tobago, and many in American schools, learn music by rote, the NIU Steelband under the direction of O'Connor, Alexis, and Teague read music scores fluently. Music literacy, in this sense, was essential to the piece Bach envisioned;[7] however, it was not until the arrival of Teague that he found his muse and felt inspired to begin writing a work for steelpan.

Bach was so taken with Teague's playing that he broke protocol and began writing the piece before money for a commission was secured.[8]

> He was, and is, a charismatic performer with complete control of his instrument and, in the words of the *Chicago Tribune* music critic, can probably play the instrument faster "than anybody can play anything." I wrote the work for Liam in the summer of 1994 after asking him if he would be interested in a work he could play with orchestra. NIU has an annual concerto concert for which our best students vie for the opportunity to play a concerto and I realized that unless Liam played a Vivaldi work, a transcription which would not be allowed in the competition, there was nothing else he could compete with. Of course, I went way overboard and wrote a twenty minute-piece.[9]

Bach was not so sure of the work's merits and fretted over the intricacies of the composition. With trepidation, he turned the finished manuscript of the concerto over to Teague during the winter of 1994–1995.

> When I wrote my harp concerto, I had a terrible time. It was a terribly difficult piece to play, simply because I didn't know my way around the harp very well. I have yet to write a guitar piece, out of the same fear. When I finished the Steelpan Concerto . . . I thought, "What have I done? Liam hasn't seen the piece. Is he going to be able to play it, or has this been a wasted exercise?" I was fortunate. He spent his Christmas vacation learning it, and when he came back he had only one request: "Can I play the second movement faster?"[10]

Teague's prodigious talent devoured the notes of Jan Bach's concerto, and mastery of the piece came in short order. Unfortunately for Teague, the work was too long to qualify for the NIU concerto competition for which it was initially written. This proved a minor issue as the work was destined for greater things; however, in the short term Teague, Bach, and others affiliated with NIU looked for venues to perform the concerto in an effort to promote Teague's virtuosity and Bach's composition. Howard Kafer, NIU School of Music chair at the time, had long sought a partnership with the Chicago Sinfonietta de Camera under the direction of conductor Paul Freeman. Bach's concerto became the focal point of a partnership between the two institutions, and preparations were made for its premiere in November of 1995.

The Chicago Sinfonietta came to the Egyptian Theatre in downtown DeKalb and performed an arrangement of the concerto with the NIU Steelband on November 11. The following night the ensemble performed the work at Rosary College in nearby River Forest, before moving to downtown Chicago for the official world premiere at Orchestra Hall on November 13. The premiere was a smashing success, and the *Chicago Tribune* hailed the concerto as "a showcase for Teague's incredible virtuosity." The music critic noted that "the audience exploded in cheers and whistles, refusing to let Teague leave the stage until he had given them a solo encore."[11] Such strong reactions have continued as Teague has continued to perform the concerto with orchestras around the world including the Sinfonia de Camera at the University of Illinois, the Peoria (Illinois) Symphony, the Saint Louis Symphony, the Buffalo (New York) Philharmonic, the Bellvue (Washington) Philharmonic, the Elmhurst Symphony, the Akron (Ohio) Symphony, the Taiwan National Symphony, the Czech National Symphony, and many others, including recently with the Elkhart (Indiana) County Symphony in March 2013. In 1999, Teague recorded the concerto with the Czech National Symphony with Paul Freeman conducting, and it was issued on the album *Exotic Concertos* a few years later.[12] On the suggestion of NIU wind ensemble conductor Dr. Ronnie Wooten, Bach created an arrangement of the steelpan concerto for wind ensemble, and Wooten conducted its premiere in 1999 with Teague as soloist.

Perhaps the biggest triumph of the collaboration between Teague and Bach was the creation of a serious piece of classical art music featuring the steelpan. Prior to the commission of the Bach concerto, Teague and other aspiring pannists were relegated to the classic violin showpieces of the nineteenth century and early twentieth century if they were to make any attempt at performing in the concert hall with a string orchestra. The steelpan, much like the marimba, the multi-percussion set-up, or the timpani, simply did not have its own repertoire, and prior to the end of the twentieth century, the transcriptions of violin works, though familiar to audiences the world over, were often clunky and unidiomatic when performed on the steelpan. Jan Bach's *Concerto for Steelpan and Orchestra* followed the precedent set by other early concertos for solo percussion instruments, such as Paul Creston's *Concertino for Marimba and Orchestra* (1940) and William Kraft's *Concerto for Timpani and Orchestra No. 1* (1983), and was a welcome addition to the medium.

As a piece of concert music, Bach's *Concerto for Steelpan and Orchestra* is a careful balance of tradition and modernity and utilizes nearly all of the tools and sound colors available to a composer working in the classical music genre in the 1990s. The work is tonal, scored for a full orchestra, and involves a full battery of ancillary percussion instruments. The concerto is set in two movements with an extended cadenza connecting the two major sections. This is no double-exposition-form, classical-era concerto of Mozart's time as the binary form of the piece is programmatic in its construction and the meaning tells a narrative that metaphorically recounts the history of the steelpan arriving on the concert stage. The first movement "Reflection" is contemplative in its lyrical quality here; in an attempt to the utilize the word "reflection" as a synonym of "pealing," which can mean "to strike or hit," Bach capitalizes on the bell tones and struck sound qualities of the steelpan. The second movement of the concerto is titled "Toccata" and is decidedly different in mood and tempo in comparison to the first movement. For this movement the composer channels the various stylistic elements from both classical and world music in an effort to, according to Bach, allow the soloist the space to "display his machine-rhythm speed, accuracy and phenomenal dynamic control; it is also a connection to [the] Baroque past."[13]

The link to the Baroque period of classical music is obvious throughout Bach's *Concerto for Steelpan*. As a stylistic period in the history of Western European classical music, the Baroque style is characterized by melodic structures that feature long, often complicated melodies frequently ornamented with trills and other musical ornaments. Contrast, whether in dynamics (volume), timbre, or musical texture, is key in this style of music. The steelpan embodies qualities that make it a perfect instrument for performing such musical heavy lifting in a full-length concerto. The long cadenza of Bach's concerto is a perfect example as it calls on the pannist to display a variety of techniques specific to the instrument, such as fast rhythmic runs, melodic touch, and harmonic and sometimes polyphonic playing.

The steelpan is a serious musical instrument with amazing capabilities that are only being discovered in the last few decades. Jan Bach's willingness to explore the steelpan as a serious instrument in a serious piece of art music is an important moment in the development of steelpan on a global scale. For anyone familiar with steelpan as it is played in Trinidad and Tobago, and by the likes of Andy Narell, Robert Greenidge and other virtuosi, the steelpan's versatility and profoundness is no secret. That said, the Jan Bach *Concerto for Steelpan and Orchestra* allows audiences geared toward classical music and critics the world over to look beyond the novelty of the instrument and to appreciate the composition's great emotional and musical depth.

> When people come up to me after a performance and say that they have never heard the pan played like that before, I usually state that what I am doing is trying to continue a tradition of highlighting the pan's musical potential that was started long before I came on the scene.[14]

In addition to the composition's Baroque sensibilities, the *Concerto for Steelpan* also exhibits the influence of several Caribbean folk-music elements such as calypso rhythms, but it should be noted, these Caribbean influences are not cheeky insertions like the Manhattan-style calypsos popular in the United States during the calypso craze of the 1950s. Context is very important; taken as a whole the *Concerto for Steelpan* by Jan Bach removes the steelpan from its traditional context in Trinidadian music and culture and instead uses the instrument in the great tradition of Western European classical-music concertos. Bach's concerto was the first of its kind, and Teague's countless performances of the work have brought the soloist and the piece onto concert stages around the world, creating a broader audience for both than had previously existed. Through his continued performances of Bach's concerto, Teague has evolved into the first legitimate concert performer of steelpan in the classical world, and to date he remains the most active and notable steelpan soloist within the genre.

Inspired by working with Bach, Teague changed his perception of his role in the world of steelpan. He now saw it as his mission to educate contemporary composers to the nuances of the steelpan, in order to foster a whole new repertoire for the instrument with enough artistic weight and compositional merit to warrant inclusion in the highest echelon of concert performances worldwide. This desire led him to commission new classical works for steelpan music. Upon taking the reins as professor of steelpan at NIU, Teague further realized that his best students did not have challenging pieces of new classical music to perform, and he has ever since worked to create and foster a repertoire for student pannists.

In 1997, a spirited Teague told *Trinidad Newsday*, "I want to show the versatility of the instrument and to master all aspects of the music. I want to be a great conductor and a great composer, to be one of the greatest musicians that has ever come out of Trinidad and Tobago."[15] Decades later, Teague's continued efforts in commissioning new works for steelpan, and mentoring and fostering interested composers and students, has taken the NIU steelband program in new directions, and since 2004 has been a key factor in establishing his own personal legacy as co-director.

The Jan Bach *Concerto for Steelpan* was an important turning point for Teague's career in the international classical-music scene, and he has since commissioned and performed a number of new works for steelpan and continues to work with some of the most eminent contemporary classical-music composers. Each time, he works to educate interested composers on the abilities of steelpan as an instrument, the range of each instrument in the steelpan family, what it can and cannot do.

Despite its importance for Teague and steelpan the Jan Bach *Concerto for Steelpan* was not, however, the pannist's introduction to classical music on steelpan, and it was O'Connor who first turned Teague on to playing classical music on steelpan.

> Al O'Connor had me work on the 2nd movement from Beethoven's 1st symphony as a student. This is what began my interest in adapting classical pieces to the steelband. Since then I have done pieces by Rossini, Tchaikovsky, Pablo de Sarasate, Saint Saens, Paganini, and even Miyagi, a Japanese composer. Generally, I choose pieces that I think will bring the audience to its feet and that provide a lot of musical contrast and interest.[16]

Grammy award–winning composer Libby Larson recalled Teague's efforts to teach her the intricacies of the steelpan. "I was at Northern Illinois University making a recording. Liam and I went to his studio and he started to play. My jaw dropped. I knew right away that I could write a piece [for the instrument], I could show off the color of the instrument.

Subsequently I have gotten to know his playing and this piece will show his brilliant stick technique."[17] Her *Concertino for Tenor Steel Drum and Chamber Ensemble* was premiered at the Birch Creek summer music academy in July of 2004.[18]

Beyond solo or mixed ensemble works featuring steelpan, Teague continues to push for new steelband works. This desire carries over into the NIU Steelband concerts held each fall and spring, which feature an impressive mix of repertoire that balances traditional calypso, new Panorama, Latin, jazz, classical, and pop arrangements. Also, since his early days at NIU, Teague has been featured with the NIU Steelband as a soloist on classical pieces and has published his own arrangements of Paganini's *Moto Perpetuo* and Rosini's *Silken Ladder Overture*.

Teague's faculty recital in the spring of 2013 featured new works for steelpan commissioned by the pannist and serves as an insightful showcase for his vision of steelpan's future at NIU and the world. The recital featured several pieces, including *Cadences*, a full-length work scored for steelpan solo and string quartet by Deborah Teason. *Cadences* is one of a small, select collection of works written for this eclectic instrumentation, and Teague performed the last two movements of this challenging work with the Avalon String Quartet. It was premiered with the Vermeer Quartet in recitals in Chicago and DeKalb in December 2006.[19] The centerpiece of the recital was three new compositions by renowned Indiana University professor of percussion Kevin Bobo.[20] The works, all commissioned by Teague, included one for steelpan solo and two duets for marimba and steelpan. NIU percussion professor Greg Byers joined Teague on one piece while Bobo, who is perhaps best known as a world-class marimbist, joined Teague on the other. Over the past several years, Teague has fostered Bobo's interest in composing for steelpan, and the composer has also written a new concerto for steelpan soloist and orchestra that Teague premiered in 2014.

The recital ended with composer Ben Wahlund's new work, *Grotesque,* inspired by the striking paintings of modern British artist Francis Bacon. In addition to composing, Wahlund is the director of the Birch Creek summer music academy and has known Teague since attending NIU in the 1990s. *Grotesque* is scored for steelpan and piano, and Teague premiered the work in Trinidad earlier in 2013. Wahlund's compositions are inspired by the composer's close connection with Teague, and he has written several other pieces for steelpan. His most notable work is *Only When Eternity Nears*, which won first prize in the inaugural International Symphony & Steel Composition Contest, run by the Music Literacy Trust of Trinidad in 2009.

The ambitious recital described above is further proof of Teague's ongoing commitment to expanding the repertoire of the steelpan for the concert stage. It is a historical fact that steelpan has faced adversity in achieving legitimacy as an appropriate musical instrument in the classical music genre, and Teague's continued work with commissioning and performing works in a classical style are working to tear down these boundaries. His efforts in this regard are an important element of his role as an educator at NIU and, paired with his own compositions and arrangements, serve to better educate his students and expand the range of steelpan into new territories.

Teague Joins the Faculty, Becomes Co-Director of the NIU Steelband

Teague's success in performing the Jan Bach steelpan concerto in the late 1990s notwithstanding, his future success as co-director of the NIU Steelband was anything but a certainty. Despite continued success as a pioneering performer of steelpan on concert stages, his education track at NIU was nearing an end in the spring of 1999. Teague was finishing his graduate degree and bracing for the reality of life after school. What would he do next? Teague's virtuosic skills as a performer were never in question, but even with two college degrees in hand, positions for pannists or steelband directors were still nonexistent in the United States. Teague was concerned about the limited opportunities if he returned home to Trinidad and feared the lack of opportunities in the United States.

With few other options, Teague returned home to Trinidad in the fall of 1999 and plotted his next move. Here, quite by accident, Teague's skills as teacher and mentor began to blossom. Initially, Teague taught steelpan part-time at various primary and secondary schools throughout Trinidad. He was considered a hero for many young Trinidadians, and talking with Trinidadian youth about future opportunities and the importance of education made an impact with the kids and the pannist. Teague's main message was one of believing in one's self: "We have so much in Trinidad to offer, our people are so creative."[21]

Throughout the year 2000, Teague continued to teach and perform relentlessly. He released his fourth album (featuring Arturo Tappin from Barbados) in the spring, performed in Italy with the sponsorship of the Angostura bitters distillery, performed at the Grenada Spice Jazz Festival, and taught during the summer at the Birch Creek summer music academy in Wisconsin and another summer steelpan camp in California.[22] That fall he appeared with the NIU Steelband for their stunning performances at the World Steel Band Music Festival competition in October.[23]

Meanwhile, while Teague was home in Trinidad, O'Connor and Alexis schemed to somehow bring the young panman back to NIU, this time in a faculty capacity. Both men agreed that Teague was to be O'Connor's successor as co-director of the NIU Steelband and professor of steelpan at NIU, but the pair was less clear about how to facilitate such a succession. The answer came via a patron of the Birch Creek summer music academy in Wisconsin, for which O'Connor was director of percussion and Teague had become a member of the steelpan faculty.

Responding to O'Connor's request for help, Birch Creek summer music academy patrons Cynthia and Carl Stiehl, in conjunction with the Miller Foundation, funded a three-year, fixed-term position for Teague at NIU under the title "research scholar."[24] The position effectively made Teague an artist-in-residence at the NIU School of Music and allowed him the opportunity to serve as an NIU faculty member in nearly every capacity from 2001 to 2004. Alexis announced the newly created position in New York in April 2001 during a ceremony in which he was honored by the Trinidad and Tobago Folk Arts Institute for his lifelong contributions to steelpan. Alexis praised NIU and the Stiehl family, boasting, "These are people who see the value of pan in a way that not even the people in the land where it was invented see it."[25]

In August of 2003, Teague officially took over the co-directorship of the NIU Steelband following O'Connor's retirement. Teague's position was still officially that of a research scholar, and it would be another two years before the tenure-track position of assistant professor of steelpan was created. Teague was eager to tackle the challenge of moving the NIU Steelband program forward, telling the *Trinidad Express*, "I want to make NIU the US Mecca of steelband and turn one of Illinois' best-kept secrets into a talking point around the world."[26] The chair of the NIU School of Music, Paul Bauer, was equally optimistic, stating, "I am very excited about the future development of the band, continuing with the important traditions, and going in new directions under a great artist."[27] In the winter of 2004, the tenure-track position previously held by O'Connor was modified in title and clarified in responsibility to reflect Teague's duties at NIU. The job was announced nationally and internationally (as is customary for university positions), and Teague applied, interviewed, and won the position. In August 2005, Teague officially assumed the position of assistant professor of steelpan at NIU and completed the transition from his predecessor and a transformation of the job. Teague blossomed in the role and through hard work and perseverance was promoted to associate professor of music in 2010 and full professor in 2016.

O'Connor made his mark at NIU by establishing, building, and nurturing the steelband program. Alexis made his stamp on the program by establishing a steelpan factory, building and supplying the band with some of the best steelpans in North America, and pushing the repertoire and rehearsal quality of the band to new heights. At the time Teague took over the NIU steelband program, the future was wide open, and O'Connor surmised, "Liam is amazingly ambitious. He really wants to move this along. We may end up with a steelband here that is 50 percent West Indian students."[28]

Teague, too, was well aware of his opportunity for personal growth, and when he officially took over the program in 2005 he knew that he would have to put his own unique stamp on the program and take it in new directions not yet seen nor heard. Into the future, Teague continues to carry the burden of steelpan's global future on his shoulders, and his exhausting performance and teaching schedule and his relentless efforts to spread steelpan around the globe are nothing short of astounding. Teague carries many of the hopes and aspirations of his country on his shoulders and takes the propagation of the steelpan seriously.

> When I first came here, to DeKalb, I was very focused on just becoming wealthy for myself, having a family, a nice house, a great car, whatever. But as the years went by, I began to think: Wait a minute. I'm in a position where I can actually take this instrument a step forward and promote my entire country. So every time I play this instrument, I don't feel as if it's just about Liam Teague or it's just about that moment. The steelpan is a national symbol of Trinidad and Tobago, and to proclaim it one of the best instruments in the world is a responsibility I must accept.[29]

Commissioning new works for steelpan solo, ensemble, and steelband was something that marked the Teague/Alexis era apart from the O'Connor/Alexis era of the NIU steelband program. Teague's interest in this pursuit began long before his ascension to the faculty ranks at NIU and is best personified by the discussion of the Bach concerto for steelpan.

In his roles as a professor of steelpan and as mentor, Teague is constantly challenging his students to perform in as many venues and situations as possible, pushing the boundaries of steelpan as an instrument. In this pursuit, Teague often leads by example. One such example is his close relationship with fellow NIU percussion faculty member Robert Chappell. Chappell is an outstanding composer, pianist, and world percussionist in his own right, and he and Teague started playing together regularly in 2000. Since then, the duo has developed a unique partnership that has led to two duet albums, *For Lack of Better Words* (2004) and *Open Windows* (2010), featuring original compositions by Teague and Chappell as well as arrangements of classical pieces by Fiocco, Bartok, and Paganini, a classic Lord Kitchener calypso, and a vintage xylophone ragtime piece by George Hamilton Green.

Not satisfied working only as a duo, Teague and Chappell expanded the group to a small combo with the addition of bass, drum set, hand percussion, and saxophone. The expanded ensemble took on the name Panoramic, recorded an album under that name, and toured the United States, Trinidad, Taiwan, and St. Lucia, using the core duo of Teague and Chappell along with favorite local musicians to fill out the group. The individual band members come from varied backgrounds and continue to perform in many other contexts. "All of the musicians bring something different musically and culturally to the table and that is one of the great things working with the band,"[30] Teague described to *The Northern Star*. The music of Panoramic was a unique world music fusion with strands from many backgrounds. Panoramic is the only "working band" that Teague has played with in his life and thus serves as an important learning experience that has added to his resources as an educator. The three albums recorded by Teague and Chappell have remained popular and show their special mutual respect and ability to work together building music that takes advantage of the wealth of their backgrounds.

Jazz in the NIU Panyard

In general, steelpan music is composed music whether taught by rote or with music, and rarely has there been much focus on pan in jazz in the history of the music in Trinidad and Tobago, though that has been changing in recent years. Indeed, there have only been a handful of pannists from the island who have emphasized jazz and improvisation. With international recording artists like jazz composer and guitarist Fareed Haque on faculty and four different jazz bands, NIU has had a strong jazz-studies program for decades. For many years, both Robert Chappell and Rich Holly taught courses in the program, and the connection between the NIU jazz program and the NIU Steelband program is strong.[31] In past concerts, the NIU Jazz Band has featured pannist Robert Greenidge, and the head of jazz studies at NIU, Ron Carter, has appeared as a guest artist on saxophone with the NIU Steelband.

Since before the arrival of Alexis in 1985, the NIU Steelband has featured the best and brightest jazz pannists in the world at their fall and spring concerts. The impressive roster includes Andy Narell, Robert Greenidge, Rudy "Two Left" Smith and Len "Boogsie" Sharpe. O'Connor saw jazz improvisation as an important skill for any serious pannist to make a career in the United States, and he, and later Alexis, gave students the opportunity to work on improvisation whenever possible. Several NIU steelpan students have gone on to success as jazz pannists. Neville York, an early steelpan major at NIU, has featured jazz improvisation in his playing for years and has performed throughout the United States and the Caribbean. Noted jazz critic Neil Tesser proclaimed York "one of only a handful of pan players able to improvise expertly."[32]

O'Connor and Alexis supported jazz improvisation as a useful tool for steelpan students; however, jazz improvisation is perhaps an even more integral component of music literacy for Teague. He feels strongly that improvisation is a necessity, and under his direction the students in the NIU steelpan program approach the technique as a required element of the curriculum, especially his graduate students. Graduate student Mike Schwebke, who has a strong interest in jazz, had jazz improvisation as a central part of his private lessons with Teague in the fall of 2013. "He is definitely focused on the 2-5-1 jazz approach, a shorter harmonic progression, and you learn thousands of patterns to go over that progression. You want to recognize that pattern in every key. And all of a sudden you can play really fast with different tunes."[33] Teague sees it as part of a larger comprehensive plan.

> Cliff and I try to create an educational environment that fosters holistic knowledge and growth. The idea is to prepare students for almost any given musical situation that they may encounter and to give them a better, deeper appreciation for other styles of music. Many of our students take individual instruction from jazz faculty and even play in jazz combos. While it is not mandatory that our students be able to improvise, I try to include improvisation in their applied lessons. Since we promote the idea of holistic growth, I try to integrate elements of improvisation in a way that would allow students to be able to use some of these concepts and approaches, even if they don't necessarily want to be seasoned improvisers.[34]

The emphasis has paid dividends for students, such as Sune Borregaard from Denmark, who come to the program with a special interest in jazz and steelpan. In 2006, Borregaard's compositions were featured in a joint concert with the NIU Steelband and Jazz Band. Teague commented, "Cliff and I approached Ron Carter [then head of jazz studies at NIU] about this. Sune had written a few jazz ensemble and steelband arrangements for one of his classes, and Cliff and I felt that it would be a good idea to have these two groups collaborate. Ron Carter was super excited about this and the rest, as they say, is history."[35]

In recent years, Teague has also brought to NIU some of the brightest young jazz improvisers on the instrument, like Victor Provost in 2010 and Leon Foster Thomas in 2011, as well as bringing back Robert Greenidge in 2013 to teach and perform. Besides inviting them as guests on the concert, he makes further use of their presence to give master classes. Provost noted that Teague made a special point to encourage his steelpan students to get a private lesson on his methodology and approach to improvisation while he was there, and as a result he gave lessons to eight or nine students.[36] Sharing the stage with the NIU Steelband is not reserved only for pannists; Teague brought Trinidad's great young jazz trumpeter Etienne Charles to DeKalb for the fall 2014 steelband concert.

Panorama, Panorama Music, and NIU

Despite his residency at NIU, Teague continues to maintain strong ties to his home in Trinidad, and in addition to trips to see family and friends, he has continued to be very involved in different aspects of the Trinidadian steelpan scene. This has included arranging works for the Panorama steelband competition during Carnival, where the best steelbands from throughout the county compete and perform complex eight-minute arrangements. The NIU Steelband spring concerts have featured performances of these Panorama-style arrangements by Alexis and other leading composers nearly every year since 1985. Teague has continued this tradition with the band, and the band has played at their spring concerts a number of his original Panorama-style compositions, including 'Chant' written in memory of Teague's late father, Russell, in 2006, those composed by Alexis, and the leading Panorama arrangements for that year.

The students of the NIU steelband program have further reaped the benefits of Teague's arranging work with Panorama. The years in which Teague has arranged for Trinidadian steelbands for Panorama, a number of NIU students have also traveled down to Trinidad to perform in his bands. These opportunities give NIU students a unique chance to experience this intensive part of the Trinidadian steelband experience. Indeed, for many pannists, being able to say they played with a band at Panorama is an important part of building credibility in the global steelpan community.

Teague's first experience arranging for Panorama came in 1990 with the Hillside Symphony steelband when he was a young man; however, since coming to NIU, Teague's more recent work has been with the San Fernando–based Skiffle Bunch Steel Orchestra during the 2004–2006 Panoramas and, more recently, Port of Spain's Starlift Steel Orchestra in 2011 and 2012.[37] Since 2014, he has arranged for the Silver Stars Steel Orchestra, where legendary arranger Edwin Pouchet designated Teague as his successor in the role of the band's arranger.

Considering Teague's training and strong background in classical music, jazz, and traditional Trinidadian steelband methods, it comes as little surprise that he has taken a strong compositional approach to panorama arranging.

> I have always viewed the Panorama "arranger" to be more of a composer than an arranger. After one arranges the original melody of a song, one basically adopts the role of a composer for the next seven, or so, minutes of the Panorama arrangement. Of course, one's compositional ideas are basically still framed around elements of the original song.[38]

While he has followed the traditional mold of arranging other people's compositions for Panorama, Teague finally broke away from the convention in 2016 with his own tune arrangement, "Panoramic." The role of arranger for Panorama comes with great responsibility in Trinidad and Tobago, and Teague has felt a strong responsibility in his new role with the Silver Stars Steel Orchestra. "The late, great Edwin Pouchet's (former arranger for Silver Stars, and the man who handpicked me to arrange for the band) philosophy was that people could elect to stay home and listen to Panorama; however, if they attended the event, he wanted to give them a performance that they would not soon forget. His credo was: "Win, lose or draw, people will always remember Silver Stars." I share his sentiment and, as a result, I wanted our entire presentation to be memorable, edifying and entertaining."[39]

Teague's progressive approach to arranging developed in earnest through his studies at NIU and stray from established approaches in Trinidadian Panorama. This approach has not always received the favor of Trinidadian steelband judges. Teague has, however, been praised by some steelpan critics in Trinidad and Tobago and elsewhere, and indeed he has been outspoken about a desire for Panorama to move away from competition to increase the creative possibilities for the music.[40] This, no doubt, is an extension of his work with the NIU steelband program. "I simply want to create music that will touch the heart, soul and intellect of the masses. If that brings Panorama victory one day, then that would be the icing on the cake."[41]

CHAPTER 12

EPILOGUE—THE NIU STEELBAND INTO THE FUTURE

> "To sum it up, if I can say in one word what I took away it was love. Both of them [Alexis and Teague] love what they do. They love the instrument. It was great working with people who love what they do. It's inspiring."
>
> —Charissa Granger[1]

From its humble beginning in 1973, the NIU Steelband has continually evolved over the course of the past forty years. In the last decade, the NIU steelband program continued to move forward under the direction of Teague and Alexis. The reputation of Liam Teague as an international star in the world of steelpan serves as an important draw, and the NIU steelband program remains one of only a few degree-granting programs in the world that offer a steelpan major. The complexity of the music and the playing level of the band has continually increased over the years, to the point that one can rightly say by any measure that the NIU Steelband is one of the best steelbands in the world.

Lester Trilla Scholarship

One constant force behind the NIU steelband program since the mid-1990s has been the patronage of Lester Trilla. By the time of O'Connor's retirement in 2003, Trilla and his philanthropic foundation had already given a substantial amount of financial support and scholarships to the NIU steelband program. Many of the scholarship recipients are from the

FIGURE 12.1. Cliff Alexis, Les Trilla, Al O'Connor (1999)

Caribbean. O'Connor is quick to acknowledge the vital role that Trilla has played over more than a decade as the primary patron for the steelband program at NIU. "A whole bunch of students were given an opportunity they never would have had because he did this. Now they're back in their home countries, contributing to the development of the arts there," O'Connor said. "Their abilities have enhanced the quality of the group, and the interaction of the students from all these different cultures has been a benefit to everybody."[2]

Nearly two decades after he first discovered the NIU Steelband, the number of Trilla scholars has nearly tripled, and his generosity and dedication to the NIU steelband program has been unwavering. Because of Trilla and the NIU/UWI–St. Augustine partnership, the current Teague/Alexis era of the NIU Steelband enjoys a steady influx of talent from the Caribbean, especially a number of graduate students who came out of the UWI undergraduate music programs. As Teague and Alexis look to the future, the diversity and quality of the NIU Steelband has never been greater, thanks in no small part to the generosity of Lester Trilla.

All University Steelband

The role of graduate students in the NIU steelband program has increased dramatically in the past decade. Normally, there are approximately three or four steelpan graduate students working on either performance certificates or master's degrees at any given time. With the influx of a larger number of steelpan majors (especially graduate students) in the early 2000s, came the need for opportunities for prospective steelpan majors to lead steelbands. Discussions between the faculty and students led to the creation of the All University Steelband in 2001. The band is open enrollment and inclusive, and no longer did students interested in steelpan need to be music majors and pass an audition to participate—as required for the NIU Steelband—as the All University Steelband was open to anyone in the university, regardless of experience level. The creation of this band expanded opportunities for the steelpan graduate students, who get real world experience as part of their education at NIU. Steelpan graduate students are encouraged to feature and rehearse their own arrangements and compositions with the All University Steelband, and the band is an invaluable resource for students of all skill levels at NIU.

To say the least, Teague and Alexis have a close working relationship with the steelpan graduate students and work together to create a unique situation for their students:

> Cliff and I have dedicated ourselves toward educating the students in a holistic manner. Many of them enter the program with obvious strengths in certain musical departments and lack proficiency in others. As a result they are exposed not only to an environment that helps them to develop their performing skills, but also one in which they can learn about steelpan tuning and building, arranging, composing, etc. What they ultimately do with the knowledge they acquire is really up to them.[3]

What they have done with the steelpan majors, especially the graduate students, is to train a new generation of pannists—many of whom have gone on to become leaders of their new generation of steelpan performers and educators, spreading the gospel of steelpan to a growing audience across the globe. With a shift toward the inclusion of more music education majors in the NIU Steelband, the mission of putting qualified steelpan teachers in the primary and secondary schools, as well as in the colleges and universities of Illinois, America, and the Caribbean, is steadily making strides.

NIU Community School of the Arts Steelband

Over the years the number of steelbands in the NIU steelband program has varied from one to three. Originally there was just one steelband, for which an audition was required; however, the popularity of this singular steelband in the 1980s led O'Connor to add another steelband for less experienced players to learn the instrument while still participating in the full steelband experience. In 2012, Teague and Alexis decided to add another steelband to the NIU steelband program for a total of three bands.[4] The most recent addition to the NIU steelband program is the creation of a separate steelband program as part of the NIU Community School of the Arts. Originally founded in 1988, the school is an outgrowth of the NIU College of Visual and Performing Arts and offers a variety of courses in the arts for children, teens, and adults. The NIU Community School of the Arts is popular in the DeKalb area, and with more than 500 people participating every semester, the school—steelband included—promotes artistic growth in the community.[5] The school "encourages lifelong involvement in the arts" and provides this experience regardless of one's ability to pay. In contrast to the highly selective college atmosphere of the NIU steelband program, the NIU Community School of the Arts is a place where students of all ability levels can meet to experience the arts. The NIU Community School of the Arts features a variety of services, including private and group instruction in music, theatre, and the visual arts.[6]

One objective of the NIU Steelband's mission is breaking down barriers wherever they may exist, and in this manner the NIU Community School of the Arts steelband program is a continuation of the NIU Steelband's mission to extend its stewardship of steelbands and steelpan outside the main campus of the university. The NIU Community School of the Arts steelband further offers current NIU Steelband members the opportunity to enhance their pedagogical skills while working with less experienced pannists. In addition to sharing the joy of steelband with others, the NIU Community School of the Arts steelband provides real-life teaching experience for NIU Steelband members, thus fostering the program's goals of spreading steelpan around the globe.

The steelband program of the NIU Community School of the Arts is directed by NIU Steelband alumna Yuko Asada, who also leads secondary-school programs in the area. Through her work, the mission of the NIU steelband program is now available to community members and nonstudents alike in DeKalb and the surrounding area. Furthermore,

FIGURE 12.2. NIU Steelband at Virginia Beach, PANFest (2016)

the NIU Community School of the Arts steelband is, in many ways, a model for the future spread of steelband in various regions throughout the United States and the world. The program extends the reach of the NIU steelband program beyond the campus walls and is one of a long list of facets of the NIU steelband program attempting to spread steelband in nonconventional ways.

Steelpan Ambassadors to the World

Over the years countless NIU steelband students have been bitten by the pan jumbie, and they too, like Al O'Connor, Cliff Alexis, and Liam Teague, have become global ambassadors for the instrument. Their accomplishments are many and as diverse as the students themselves. This includes the likes of Jeffrey Thomas Ross, who published the first discography on steelband in addition to completing his graduate thesis focused on steelband history.[7] In Trinidad and Tobago several faculty members of the University of the West Indies–St. Augustine—Harold Headley, Satanand Sharma, and Jeannine Remy—are NIU alumni. Recent graduates Khion de Las and Barry Mannette are both teaching in various settings in Trinidad, as is Natalie Gonzalez. Seion Gomez is one of the most sought-after arrangers for small, medium, and large steelband for Panorama and Carnival in Trinidad and Tobago, Brooklyn, and Notting Hill, London.

NIU Steelband alums are active elsewhere in the Caribbean. Gay Magnus has become perhaps the leading steelpan pedagogue in Jamaica, where she works with numerous steelbands and has written two steelband teaching guides. Neville York is the Director of Culture in St. Maarten and is still involved with steelbands on the island. Khan Cordice has earned accolades for his work with steelbands throughout the Caribbean, and his arrangements for the Hell's Gate Steel Orchestra have won the Antigua Panorama five times since 2009. After joining the NIU Steelband in 1986, Paulette Frazier-Alexis later went on to earn a degree in law. She is now an attorney in the Virgin Islands and works with the St. Croix Rising Stars Steelband.

There are NIU Steelband graduates spread from near to far around the United States. In Illinois, Paul Ross founded the Elgin Community College Steel Band and now leads the Harper College Steelband. Frank Check teaches steelband at Waubonsee Community College in Sugar Grove, Illinois. His predecessor in that position was Elizabeth DeLamater, another NIU steelband alumni, who is now teaching steelpan in Ohio. Kenneth Joseph works full-time in New Haven, Connecticut teaching steelpan in school, community, and church steelbands. Leonard Moses teaches percussion and steelband at Central State University in Ohio and has been there for over twenty years. Talib Robinson is teaching and performing steelpan in Toronto, while Sune Borregaard is teaching and playing steelpan in Copenhagen. After completing her graduate degree at NIU, Sophia Subero served as the executive director of the Virginia Rhythm Project steelband program and PANorama Caribbean Music Festival. Josanne Francis has served as the Artistic Coordinator for CAFÉ (Cultural Academy for Excellence) since 2014, where she teaches steelpan to youth in the

Washington, DC area. In 2016, Mia Gormandy was appointed Assistant Professor of Steelpan at the University Trinidad and Tobago. Currently, several other students (such as David Aarons at the University of Washington) who earned graduate degrees in steelpan are now working toward doctorates in ethnomusicology.

Webcasting to the World

Without leaving the friendly confines of DeKalb, the NIU Steelband is now reaching an international audience via live webcasts. All NIU School of Music concerts and recitals held at the Boutell Memorial Concert Hall and the adjacent recital hall are broadcast live via the Internet and are viewed by steelpan enthusiasts around the world. The NIU Steelband's high-tech live high-definition webcasts are shot by experienced NIU student recording engineers, who control four robotic cameras. The experience of the webcast is second only to actually being present, and the viewer feels as if he is right there in the concert hall. Indeed, the NIU School of Music is very proud of its setup for webcasting live student music performances. The NIU head of recording services, Dan Nichols, notes, "Our webcasts have been seen in over 150 countries on 6 continents and our YouTube channel has nearly 1000 videos and almost one million video views."[8] The NIU webcasts have become very popular with serious steelpan fans around the world. Over 1,300 fans saw the spring 2013 NIU Steelband concert via the web, and the numbers for future concert webcasts is sure to grow each year.[9]

The popular blog and online steelband community billboard When Steel Talks regularly reviews the NIU Steelband concert webcasts. As part of its positive review of the webcast of the 2010 concert, When Steel Talks noted the far reach of the NIU Steelband: "The concert was a huge success both in terms of musical performances and technological outreach." The feedback on the When Steel Talks (WST) network, which also carried the web broadcast live, was extremely positive. Many steelpan music fans and people in the music industry watched the show from all over the world. Indeed, one WST network watcher was so impressed with the NIU Steelband performance that he now wants to attend NIU.[10]

The live webcasts allow the numerous supporters and alumni of the NIU Steelband, especially those in Trinidad and Tobago, the ability to follow the latest developments of the band from afar. The groundbreaking work of the NIU Steelband is no longer a secret, and the live webcasts allow the world an opportunity to experience the latest developments and performances of the band.

Awards for the Teague/Alexis NIU Steelband

In the last several years, the international stature of the NIU steelband program was greatly enhanced by awards for both of the band's co-directors. In November 2006, Alexis and the other members of the Trinidad and Tobago National Steel Orchestra were honored for their groundbreaking work back in 1965 by the Ministry of Community Development, Culture and Gender Affairs in partnership with Pan Trinbago.[11] In 2009, Alexis was honored with an outstanding service award from NIU.[12] In 2012, Alexis received two Emmy awards for his work on *Hammer on Steel*, a documentary produced at the University of Akron, for which Alexis was a key consultant.[13] As part of a tremendous honor that recognizes his entire career in steelpan, Alexis was inducted into the Percussive Arts Society Hall of Fame in 2013.[14] The Percussive Arts Society noted his contributions in a glowing tribute.

> Clifford Alexis has come to represent quality and innovation for steelpan builders, tuners, educators, performers, and aficionados. He is known the world over as a steelpan builder/tuner of the highest echelon, a skilled performer, a creative composer and arranger, and one with a natural ability to teach and inspire students from all walks of life.[15]

Not to be outdone, Al O'Connor, too, was celebrated for his contribution to the greater percussion community and was honored with the 2014 Lifetime Achievement in Education award by the Percussive Society for his contributions to steelband and percussion education in the United States.

In 2000, Teague won the Outstanding Young Alumni Award from the NIU Alumni Association.[16] In 2010, he was given a special award at the National Junior Panorama by the Trinidad and Tobago Ministry of Education & Pan Trinbago and Pan in Schools Coordinating Council. At the PASIC fiftieth anniversary convention in Indianapolis, he was featured as a soloist with the mass steelband put together for the special occasion. The NIU Steelband first brought steelpan to PASIC decades prior and had since enjoyed a continual presence at the international percussion community's most important annual gathering. In 2012, the Trinidadian government, on the occasion of the fiftieth anniversary of Trinidad and Tobago's independence, conferred perhaps the greatest award ever bestowed upon Teague. He was awarded the Silver Hummingbird Medal, one of the country's highest honors.[17] In 2014, Teague was awarded perhaps his most prestigious prize, the Anthony Sabga Caribbean Award for Excellence in Arts and Letters. The award celebrates the achievements of Teague on a Caribbean-wide level and is probably the most prestigious arts award available in the region at large.

NIU Steelband Into the Future

Throughout the pages of this book, the authors have chronicled the vast works and developments of the NIU steelband program. From Al O'Connor, to Cliff Alexis, to Liam Teague, to the multitude of students, the history of the program is a unique tapestry woven with the vision and experiences of a cast of thousands. The NIU Steelband continues to play to new audiences in the Midwest and across the United States, including PANFest 2016 in Virginia Beach, Virginia.[18]

Looking to the past has illuminated many amazing stories, and the words of O'Connor, Alexis, Teague, their colleagues, and NIU students tell an account of the NIU Steelband befitting the band's international reputation for excellence and musicianship. It is perhaps appropriate, then, that we turn to the words of current NIU Steelband directors Liam Teague and Cliff Alexis for their vision and hopes for the future of the NIU steelband program. Teague, for one, is very much interested in the musical and pedagogical progress:

> I hope that the NIU steelband program will eventually develop to the point where undergraduate and graduate students, on an even larger scale, will attend. While we have had an impressive roster of students, both in terms of quality and quantity, I am thinking on a more astronomical level. There are many across the globe who are still not aware of our program, so I want NIU to become a household name. I also hope that we will be able to hire additional faculty who possess expertise in areas such as steelpan history and research. We also want to continue to foster an environment which encourages creativity without borders. Cliff and I feel so fortunate to have our own "laboratory" in the NIU steelband and steelpan studio, where we can create without any inhibition. I'd also like for our band to collaborate with as many different types of musicians and ensembles as possible. One of our mantras is to break down barriers, and this would certainly be consistent with our message. I'd love for us to be in a position to provide even more scholarships to deserving musicians around the world.[19]

Alexis's hope for the future of the NIU steelband program revolves around the instrument and its spread throughout the world. He notes that "hopefully, the program will keep growing and growing; and will continue to educate future steelpan teachers and performers of this wonderful instrument."[20]

Since the introduction of the steelband at NIU in 1973, many institutions of higher learning in the United States have formed their own steelbands. None, however, has done so quite to the level and accomplishment of the NIU Steelband. The NIU Steelband has flourished where other steelband programs failed, and this is due in no small part to the talent and dedication of Al O'Connor, Cliff Alexis, Liam Teague, and a plethora of NIU students, staff, and NIU's administration. The NIU steelband program's present is bright, but the future, like that of music programs everywhere, is somewhat uncertain. Yet if past performances are any predictor of future results, the NIU steelband program is sure to innovate and lead the next generation of pannists and steelband arrangers in the United States and beyond. The first forty years of the NIU steelband program have been an unquestionable success, and the next forty years will surely be more of the same.

APPENDIX ONE

NIU STEELBAND RECORDINGS

NIU Steelband: Calypso, Pop & Classics (1977)

Side One

"The Happy Wanderer"
"Kids Medley"
"J. S. Bach: Air from Suite No. 3"
"Beatles Medley"
"A Trinidad Song"
"Matilda"

Side Two

"Amelia Rosa"
"Selections from Jesus Christ Superstar"
"Yellow Bird"
"Disco Medley"
(Silver Custom Crest NIU 81877 LP Album, 1977)

Real Steel (1985–1986)

Side One

1. "Rock Yuh, Pan Man" (Ray Holman), arr. by Cliff Alexis

2. "Toccata & Fugue in D Minor" (J. S. Bach), arr. & abr. by US Navy Steel Band
3. "One Note Samba" (Antonio Carlos Jobim), arr. by Joel Fox, Brad Stirtz, vibraphonist

SIDE TWO

4. "Kaeiso" (Lennard V. Moses), Andy Narell, soloist
5. "Calypso for Pan" (Cliff Alexis), comp. and arr. for "the little band" by Cliff Alexis
6. "Don't Back Back" (Slinger Francisco), arr. for Trinidad Catelli Allstars by Smooth Edwards, adap. by Al O'Connor

(Self-released, cassette only, 1986. Side one recorded live in concert, February 18, 1986. Side two cut February 17, 1985)

NIU Steelband: The 1992 Taiwan Tour (1993)

1. "Say It With Pan" (Cliff Alexis)
2. "Toccata and Fugue in D Minor" (J. S. Bach), arr. Al O'Connor (abridged)
3. "I Can't Wait Another Minute" (High Five), arr. Cliff Alexis
4. "Wood-n-Steel" (Robert Chappell)
5. "Pan Dingolay" (Lord Kitchener), arr. Cliff Alexis
6. "Adagio" (Samuel Barber), arr. Al O'Connor
7. "Confusion" (Cliff Alexis)
8. "Have You Seen Her" (The Chi-Lites), arr. Cliff Alexis
9. "Fire Down Below" (Len "Boogsie" Sharpe)

(Recorded at the Taiwan National Concert Hall, March 16, 1992. The Northern Illinois University School of Music, NITT92, 1993)

NIU Steelband: Return to Taiwan (1998)

1. "Mind Yuh Business" (Len "Boogsie" Sharpe), arr. Cliff Alexis
2. Four Movements from *Water Music* (G. F. Handel), arr. James Walker & Al O'Connor
3. "Miss You Like Crazy" (Masser, Goffin and Glass), arr. Cliff Alexis
4. "Variations Basileiras" (Robert Chappell)
5. "Generation Concerto" (Ethan O'Connor)
6. "Setempo" (I. Lins and G. Peranzetta), arr. Cliff Alexis
7. "Misbehave" (Len "Boogsie" Sharpe), arr. Cliff Alexis
8. Medley of Taiwan Folk Songs, arr. Al O'Connor, I. "The Train Song," II. "White Jasmine Flowers in the Sixth Moon"

(Liam Teague, soloist. NITT98, 1998)

NIU Steelband: Festival of Voices, 2006

1. Utsav-Ki-Awaz "Festival of Voices" (Jit Samaroo)
2. "Good Times" (Mark Loquan), arr. Cliff Alexis
3. "The Battle is the Lord's" (Yolanda Adams/Michael McKay), arr. Cliff Alexis
4. "Soledad" (Astor Piazolla), arr. Liam Teague
5. "Cantei Pra Distrair/Cade Ioio" (I sung to pass the time/Where's Ioio?) (Tio Helio/Cesar Venono)
6. "Chant" (Liam Teague)
7. "Marche Slave" (Tchaikovsky), arr. Liam Teague
8. "Mystery of Pan" (Shelton Besson/Alvin Daniel), arr. Seion Gomez

(Recorded at the spring 2006 concert on April 23, 2006)

NIU Steelband: Dangerous (2014)

1. "Pan in A Minor" (Lord Kitchener), arr. Liam Teague
2. "Song to the Chiricahua" (Cliff Alexis)
3. "Heal the World" (Michael Jackson), arr. Liam Teague
4. "Capriccio Italian" (Tchaikovsky) adap. Abe Breiling
5. "Sakura" (Japanese traditional), arr. Yuko Asada
6. "Dougla" (Liam Teague), dedicated to Jaden Teague-Nunez
7. "Tudo é Festa" (Mario Sergio Sereno), arr. Cliff Alexis
8. "Dangerous" (Mark Loquan/Ken Philmore), arr. Seion Gomez

(Recorded at the NIU School of Music 2005–2013. Self-released, 2014)

LIAM TEAGUE SOLO RECORDINGS

Hands Like Lightning (1993)

1. "Hands Like Lightning" (Liam Teague), arr. Calliston Pantor & Liam Teague
2. "Love Is" (Tonio K & John Keller), arr. Calliston Pantor & Samuel Jack
3. "Mr. Magic" (Liam Teague)
4. "Same Here" (Liam Teague)
5. "Nice" (Liam Teague)
6. "No Woman No Cry" (Bob Marley)
7. "Have I Told You Lately" (Liam Teague)
8. "A Whole New World" (Aladdin's theme), arr. Liam Teague
9. "A Visit to Hell" (Liam Teague)

(Produced by Robin Foster & Calliston Pantor. Engineer Robin Foster. Executive Producer Robert "Sack" Foster & Peter Scoon. Engine Room Recording and Production Ltd., 1993)

Emotions of Steel (1996)

1. "Donna Lee" (Charlie Parker)
2. "Night In Tunisia" (Dizzy Gillespie and Frank Paparelli)
3. "Pan Is Meh Jumbie" (Robert Greenidge)
4. "Here's That Rainy Day" (Jimmy Van Heusen and Johnny Burke)
5. "Blue Bossa" (Kenny Dorham)
6. "Green Dolphin Street" (Bronisław Kaper and Ned Washington)
7. "Feels So Good" (Chuck Mangione)
8. "Take A Break Today" (Len "Boogsie" Sharpe)
9. "Oh Yes I Remember Clifford" (Manhattan Transfer)
10. "Summer Song" (Cliff Alexis)
11. "Raindrops" (Liam Teague)

(Produced by Ovid Alexis & Robin Foster. Executive Producer Robert "Sack" Foster & Robin Foster. Engine Room Recording and Production Ltd., ERP9603, 1996)

Impressions (1998)

1. "Jammin'" (B. Marley)
2. "Tico Tico" (J. G. Abreu)

3. "Crying" (Len "Boogsie" Sharpe)
4. "Pan Night and Day" (Lord Kitchener)
5. "High Mass" (David Rudder)
6. "Oh What A Friend We Have In Jesus" (C. Alman)
7. "Ven, Devórame Otra Vez" (P. Hernandez)
8. "88 In the Shade" (R. Chappell)
9. "Tanga" (J. Gillespe)
10. "Lately" (S. Wonder)
11. "Steel Band Times" (A. Tanker)
12. "Impressions" (L. Teague)

(Executive Producer Robert "Sack" Foster & Robin Foster. Engine Room Recording and Production, Ltd., 1998)

T'nT Teague/Tappin (2000)

1. "T'nT"
2. "D' Hammer"
3. "Pump Me Up"
4. "D' Kid"
5. "Tobago"
6. "Thank You Kitchie"
7. "The Closer I get to You"
8. "J.G."
9. "1990"
10. "Chrome"
11. "De Road"

(With Barbadian Saxophonist Arturo Tappin. Engine Room Recording and Production Ltd., 2000)

Liam Teague + Robert Chappell, For Lack of Better Words (2002)

1. "Allegro" (J. H. Fiocco)
2. "Six Dances in Bulgarian Rhythm (I)" (Bela Bartok)
3. "Six Dances in Bulgarian Rhythm (VI)" (Bela Bartok)
4. "Moto Perpetuo" (Niccolo Paganini)
5. "For Lack of Better Words" (Robert Chappell)
6. "In One Breath" (Robert Chappell)
7. "Panoraga" (Robert Chappell)
8. "The Honeybee" (Liam Tague)
9. "Triplets" (George Hamilton Green)
10. "Pan Dingolay" (Lord Kitchener)

(Produced by Robert Chappell and Liam Teague. Rhythmic Union Records R4867, 2002)

A Christmas Gift (2002)

1. Medley—Carols (traditional): "Rudolph the Red-Nosed Reindeer," "Frosty the Snow Man," "Here Comes Santa Claus," "Jingle Bells," "Santa Claus Is Coming to Town"
2. Medley—Parang (traditional): "Las Pasqualidad," "Allegrea," "Trini Christmas," "Din Din Din," "O La De Lamar"
3. "Come Go"
4. "Every Year, Every Christmas"

5. "The Christmas Song" (Chestnuts)
6. "Ave Maria" (Schubert)
7. "Ave Maria" (Bach)
8. "Give Love on Christmas Day"
9. Medley—Christmas Songs: "Let It Snow," "Cherry Lane," "Sleigh Ride," "Jingle Bell Rock," "Winter Wonderland"
10. "Soca Santa"
11. "O Holy Night"
12. "Have Yourself a Merry Little Christmas"

(Produced by Liam Teague. Sack Records sac002, 2002)

Panoramic: Rhythm Through the Unobstructed View (2005)

1. "Panoramic" (Liam Teague)
2. "Orlando's *Cha Cha*" (Robert Chappell)
3. "Chant" (Liam Teague)
4. "Ivory Coast" (Robert Chappell)
5. "88 Degrees in the Shade" (Robert Chappell)
6. "Pearls" (Liam Teague)
7. "Nikkara" (Robert Chappell)
8. "Calcados Feliz" (Robert Chappell)

(Rhythmic Union Records RU4868, 2005)

Liam Teague + Robert Chappell, Open Window (2010)

1. "Open Window" (Robert Chappell)
2. "Sanchari" (Robert Chappell)
3. "El Rio" (Liam Teague)
4. "Branches of Snow" (Robert Chappell)
5. "Dougla" (Liam Teague)
6. "Cell O' Vibes" (Liam Teague)
7. "Calypsonata" (Liam Teague)
8. "True North" (Ben Wahlund)
9. "Introduction and Rondo Capriccioso" (Camille Saint-Saens)
10. "Spickle" (Liam Teague)
11. "Branches of Snow" (Reprise) (Robert Chappell)

(Rhythmic Union Records R4867, 2010)

LIAM TEAGUE RECORDINGS ON ANTHOLOGY

Concerto for Steelpan and Orchestra (Jan Bach, composer)
Czech National Symphony Orchestra (Paul Freeman, conductor, Liam Teague, steelpan. On *Paul Freeman Introduces Exotic Concertos*. Albany 521, 2002)

LIAM TEAGUE RECORDINGS WITH OTHER GROUPS

James Walker, *Rhyme or Reason* JWG-2003, 2000
St. Luke's Steelband with Liam Teague, 2008

APPENDIX TWO

Compositions, Arrangements and Commissions for Steelpan (current as of 2013)

ARRANGEMENTS BY AL O'CONNOR FOR STEELBAND (AN INCOMPLETE LIST)

"Afternoon Tears," 1986
"Adagio" (Barber), 1990/1991
"All My Trials," 1992/93
"All Night Long"
"Anna"
Appalachian Spring (Copland), 1987/88
"Aria" from *Suite No. 3 in D* (Bach), 1977, recorded by the NIU Steelband, 1977
"Battle Hymn of the Republic," 1990/91
"Beatles Medley," 1974, recorded by the NIU Steelband, 1977
"Birdland," 1978
"Black Is the Color of My True Love's Hair"
Brandenberg Concerto No. 3, 1st Mvt., 1979, rev. 1986
"Bridge Over Troubled Water," 1982, revised 1980
"Brute Force," 1978
"Calypso Music" (David Rudder), 1987/88, arranged for Ed Soph
"Canon for Strings," 1983
"Changes," 1987
"Children's Medley," 1977, recorded by the NIU Steelband, 1977
"Coka Yoka," 1976
"Conga," 1986
"The Death of Ase," (Edvard Grieg)

"Disco Medley," 1975, recorded by the NIU Steelband, 1977
"Don't Back Back" (Sparrow), 1985
"Don't Leave Me This Way" (Gamble/Huff), 1979
"Evergreen," 1980
"Everybody Loves Saturday Night," 1973, recorded by the University of Illinois Steelband, 1981
"Everybody Wants to Go to Heaven"
"Fantasy," 1978
Finale from *Symphony No. 5* (Shostakovich), 1989/90
"Fire Fire" (Calypso Rose) 1973
"Fret Not Thyself," 1984
"Good Neighbors All," 1981
"Guitars and Tiki Bars"
"Happy Wanderer," 1973, recorded by the NIU Steelband, 1977
"Hello Africa/Africa," 1982
"I Just Called to Say I Love You" (Stevie Wonder)
"In the Hall of the Mountain King" (Edvard Grieg), 1992/93
"Is This Love," 1978, rev. 1992/93
"Jesus Christ Superstar," 1977, recorded by the NIU Steelband, 1977
"Jovial Jasper," 1983
"Joy," 1985
"J'taime"
"Late in the Evening"
"Magogany," 1976
"Malaguena," 1979
"Marijuana", 1975, recorded by the NIU Steelband, 1977
"Mas in Madison Square Garden," 1981
"Mas in May" (Kitchener), recorded by the University of Akron Steelband, 1977
"Me and Julio"
"Morning Stretch," 1984
Overture to *Carmen* (Bizet), 1977, rev. 1986
Overture to *Egmont* (Beethoven), 1992/93
"Pan on the Run" (Holman), 1983
"Pan Rising," 1987
"Party Time," 1987
"The Peace Carol," 1979
The Pines of Rome (Ottorino Respighi), 2003
"Please Don't Leave Me This Way," 1979, rev 1985
"Power," 1985
"Sabre Dance" (Khatchaturian), 1977
"Sand," 1986
"Scarlet Begonias"
"Settle Me Down"
"Sinking Ship" (Gypsy), 1987/88, rev 1988/89, arranged for drummer Ed Soph
"Sir Duke," 1976
"So Bad," 1984
"Soca Medley," 1983
"Soul Chick," 1980
"Stir It Up," 1984
"The Strayaway Child" (Michael Gorman), 1985

"Sunset," 1987
"Sweet Mary in the Morning"
Symphony No. 5, Mvt. 4 (Shostakovich), ?
"Tempo"
"Three Little Birds," 1992/93
"Too Young to Soca," 1987
"Tropical Allusions" (Andy Narell), 1985
"Try Jah Love," 1985
Water Music (Handel), 1980, 1997
"Under the Sea," 1992/93
"Walk and Don't Look Back," 1978
"Way of the World," 1978
"When the Sun Goes Down"
"Where the Boat Leaves From"
"Mother and Child Reunion," 1978

Compositions by Cliff Alexis for Steelpan

"Confusion Reggae," 2002
"It Is"
"Keep Yuh Focus" (Sweet T n T), 2007
"Keth It"
"Luv It"
"Pan Is It," 1997
"Pan 2000," Pan Press, 2000
"Plenty Pan," 1998
"Summer Song," Pan Press
"Tell Me"
"What If," 2005

Arrangements by Cliff Alexis for Steelpan

"As" (Stevie Wonder), c. 2010
"The Battle is the Lord's" (Yolanda Adams), 2006
"Cantei Pra Distrair/Cade Ioio" (I Sung to Pass Time/Ioio's Wish) (Tio Helio/Cesar Venono), 2006
"Canto Meier" (The Song of Songs) (Cruz/Sombrinha/Portela)
"Chega de Saudade" (No More Blues) (Antonio Jobim), c. 2009
"Colours" (Lincoln "Fats" Waldron, Alvin Daniel) 2002
"Good Times" (Mark Loquan), 2006
"I Can't Wait Another Minute" (High Five), 1998
"I Wish" (Stevie Wonder), c. 2009
"If I Ain't Got You" (Alicia Keys), 2005
"Magic Drum" (Sharpe), c. 2009
"Mind Your Business" (Len "Boosie" Sharpe), 1997
"Miracle" (L. A. Reid & Babyface), 1993
"Misbehave" (Len "Boosie" Sharpe), 1997
"Miss You Like Crazy" (Masser, Goffin & Glass), 2002
"Music For the Soul" (Hollis Wright), c. 2004
"Music in We Blood" (Len "Boosie" Sharpe), c. 2004

"Mystery Band" (Lord Kitchener), 1993
"Pan History" (Orville Wright), 2005
"Pandora" (De Fosto), c. 2004
"The Path" (Ralph MacDonald), 2006
"Push My Pan" (Roger Boothman, Alvin Daniel), 2002
"Rock Yuh, Pan Man" (Ray Holman), 1986
"Ruction" (Jason "Peanuts" Isaac/Ingrid DePeiza), 2011
"Savannah Party" (David Rudder), 1993
"Setembro" (Gilson Peranzetta And Ivan Lins), 2003
"Ten Commandments of Pan" (Jason "Peanut" Isaac), 2008
"Tudo e Festa" (Sereno/Mario Sergio), 2005
"War 2004" (De Fosto), 2005
"We Are in This Love Together" (Al Jarraeu), 2011
"What Kind of Man Would I Be," 1997
"Woman's Worth" (Alicia Keys), 2002

Compositions by Liam Teague for Pan

"Calypsonata" for steelband, 2007, published by Akron: MauMauMusic, performed at 2002 Spring Concert by the NIU Steelband
"Cell o Vibes" for cello steelpan, 2007, published by Akron: MauMauMusic
"Chant," composition for steelband, 2006, published by Denver: Ramajay Music
"Dougla" for steelband, 2008, published by Denver: Ramajay Music
"El Rio" for soprano steelpan, 2008, published by Akron: MauMauMusic
"The Firebrand," not published, c. 1989
"The Honey Bee," for soprano steelpan, Pan Press
"Impressions," Pan Press, 1998
"Love" for soprano steelpan, 2008, published by Akron: MauMauMusic
"Panoramic," 2015
"Pearls," not published
"Raindrops," for soprano steelpan, Pan Press
"Spickle" for soprano steelpan and steelband, 2006, published by Akron: MauMauMusic
"Tryin ah ting" for soprano steelpan, 2008, published by Akron: MauMauMusic
"A Visit to Hell" for soprano steelpan, Pan Press

Arrangements by Liam Teague for Steelpan

"Ashley" (Len "Boogsie" Sharpe), c. 2007
"Colours Again" (Mark Loquan/ Ken "Professor" Philmore/Destra Garcia), for TCL Group Skiffle Bunch, 2006
"Conscious Chutney" (Ras Shorty I), 2007
"Fuego Contra Fuego" (Mariano Perez/Carlos Gomez), 2007
"Haru no Umi" (Miyagi), 2008, published by Akron: MauMauMusic
"Heal the World" (Michael Jackson), c. 2010
"How Great Thou Art" (traditional), 2008, published by Akron: MauMauMusic
"In She Rainorama" for Starlift Steel Orchestra (Original DeFosto Himself), 2011
"Introduction and Rondo Capriccioso" (Saint Saens), 2007
"Marche Slave" (Tchaikovsky), Pan Press, 2006
"Moto Perpetuo" (Paganini), 2008, published by Akron: MauMauMusic

"Nostalgia" (Mark Loquan), c. 2007
"Pan in A Minor" (Kitchener), 2008, published by Akron: MauMauMusic for TCL Group Skiffle Bunch for the World Steelband Music Festival, Madison Square Garden, New York
"Pan Night and Day" (Lord Kitchener) for TCL Group Skiffle Bunch, 2005
"Rewind" (Mark Loquan), c. 2010
Silken Ladder "Overture" (Rossini), 2008, published by Akron: MauMauMusic
"Soledad" (Astor Piazolla), 2006
"Steelband Times" (Andre Talker), c. 2010
Symphony No. 1 (Beethoven), 2003
"Vibes" (Mark Loquan/ Ken "Professor" Philmore/Destra Garcia) for Starlift Steel Orchestra, 2012
"War 2004" for TCL Group Skiffle Bunch (Original DeFosto Himself), 2004
"Zigeunerweisen" (Pablo de Sarasate), c. 2008

Compositions commissioned by/for the NIU Steelband or Liam Teague

Jan Bach, *Concerto for Steelpan and Orchestra*
Jan Bach, "Songs of the Streetwise" for choir and steelband, [2001?]
Kevin Bobo, "Ezekiel's Wheel"
Kevin Bobo, "Friday," [2013?]
Kevin Bobo, *Origins and Expansions*, concerto for steelpan and wind ensemble, 2013
Kevin Bobo, "Three Rings," 2013
Robert Chappell, "Wood-n-Steel," 1992
Robert Chappell, "Nikkara," c. 2010
Michael Colgrass, *Pan Trio* for steelpan, percussion and harp, 2008
David Gordon, "Studies on the Pythagorean Gong," for soprano steelpan, 2013
Libby Larsen, Concertino for steelpan and chamber ensemble
Erik Ross, "Echo" for steelpan and brass ensemble, 2009
Deborah Fischer Teason, *Cadences* for steelpan and string quartet, 2006
Ben Wahlund, Grotesque for steelpan and piano, 2013
Ben Wahlund, *Only When Eternity Nears* for steelpan and orchestra, 2009
Ben Wahlund, "True North" for steelpan, percussion, and piano

NOTES

NOTES TO CHAPTER 1

1. Press release, "NIU Steel Band to Celebrate Three Decades with Special Concert," *NIU News*, March 31, 2003.

2. Liam Teague, interview by Andrew Martin, November 17, 2012.

3. The US military confined its efforts to Trinidad and did not have any tangible base or presence on Trinidad's sister island of Tobago.

4. For information on the American occupation of Trinidad during WWII, see Harvey Neptune, *Caliban and the Yankees: Trinidad and the United States Occupation* (Chapel Hill: University of North Carolina Press, 2007).

5. Kim Johnson, interview with Andrew Martin, February 22, 2011, Port of Spain, Trinidad. See also Stephen Stuempfle, *The Steelband Movement: The Forging of A National Art in Trinidad and Tobago* (Philadelphia: University of Pennsylvania Press, 1995), 76–140, and George Goddard *Forty Years in the Steelbands 1939–1979*, ed. Roy D. Thomas (London: Karia Press, 1991).

6. Molly Ahye, *Cradle of Caribbean Dance: Beryl McBurnie and the Little Carib Theatre*. (Trinidad and Tobago: Heritages Cultures, 1983), 48.

7. Andrew Martin and Ray Funk, "Show Me the Music: A Brief History of Pan Music Notation," in *Proceedings of the International Conference and Panorama 2015*, ed. Andrew Martin and Ray Funk (St. Augustine, Trinidad: University of the West Indies Press, forthcoming).

8. Stuempfle, *Steelband Movement*, 101.

9. For more information on the calypso craze, see Ray Funk and Michael Eldridge, *Calypso Craze*, Bear Family BCD 16947, 2014.

10. The most important of these was the Hart-Cellar Act, which abolished the National Origins Formula that restricted the influx of immigrants based on existing percentages of an ethnic group's population present in the United States at any given time. The National Origins Formula was first enacted in 1924 and effectively set low immigration quotas for several geographic areas including Eastern Europe and the Caribbean, whose citizens, prior to the act, enjoyed relatively easy immigration access to the United States.

11. Ted Solís, "Teaching What Cannot Be Taught: An Optimistic Overview," in *Performing Ethnomusicology*, ed. Ted Solís (Berkeley: University of California Press, 2004), 7.

12. Brandon Haskett, "Thoughts on Multicultural Music Education and Creativity," "Brandon Haskett's Music Education Blog," accessed September 22, 2013, http://blhaskett.wordpress.com/steelpan-research/.

13. See Solís. "Teaching What Cannot Be Taught." See also Brandon Haskett, "They Came for the Kids and Stayed for the Teacher: The Desert Winds Community Steel Orchestra," *International Journal of Community Music* 6, no. 2 (July 2013): 175–82; and Brandon Haskett, "A Study of U.S. Collegiate and K–12 Steel Band Directors' Attitudes Regarding Steel Band Curriculum and Pedagogy," *Update: Applications of Research in Music Education* 34, no. 2 (2016): 5–12.

14. Andrew R. Martin, "A Voice of Steel through the Iron Curtain: Pete Seeger's Contributions to the American Steel Band Movement," *American Music* 29, no. 3 (Fall 2011): 353–80.

NOTES TO CHAPTER 2

1. Kuo-Huang Han, e-mail to Andrew Martin, March 18, 2013.
2. Al O'Connor, interview by Andrew Martin, November 6, 2014.
3. Al O'Connor, telephone interview by Andrew Martin, October 16 2012.
4. Al O'Connor, interview by Satanand Sharma, November 6, 2000.
5. *Electronic Music from the University of Illinois,* MGM/Heliodor H/HS-25047, 1967.
6. Ibid.
7. Al O'Connor, e-mail to Andrew Martin, March 27, 2013.
8. Bill Bass, "About," "Bill Bass Steel Pans," accessed October 28, 2013, http://billbasssteelpans.com/about/.
9. They recorded one album in 1969. See "Mike Alexander and The Pott Steelers—Virgin Islands Beach Party," "Discogs," accessed March 10, 2016, https://www.discogs.com/Mike-Alexander-And-The-Pott-Steelers-Virgin-Islands-Beach-Party/release/3068872.
10. "Steelband Makes First Recording," *Virgin Island Daily News*, August 13, 1966.
11. Al O'Connor, interview by Andrew Martin, November 16, 2012.
12. This number is based on a reading of issues of *Percussive Notes* from the decade of the 1970s.
13. "Electric Stereopticon," Annex Group, accessed March 29, 2013, http://www.annexgroup.org/blog/?page_id=15.
14. See liner notes to the Cook recordings from mid-1950s, Emory Cook, *Brute Force Steel Band of Antigua*, Cook 01042, 1955.
15. Andrew R. Martin, *Military Might, Melodious Music: The United States Navy Steel Band 1957–1999* (Oxford: University of Mississippi Press, 2016).
16. Al O'Connor, interview by Andrew Martin, November 16, 2012.
17. Kuo-Huang Han, e-mail to Andrew Martin, March 20, 2013.
18. Musica Exotica III program and program notes, April 1–3, 1977.
19. Michael Bento, e-mail to Jeannine Remy, March 10, 2013.
20. Jeff Bush, e-mail to Andrew Martin, October 3, 2012.
21. Al O'Connor, interview by Andrew Martin, November 16, 2012.

NOTES TO CHAPTER 3

1. Al O'Connor, Graduate School Project Grant report 1979, NIU Steel Band Archive.
2. Cliff Alexis, interview by Andrew Martin, November 16, 2012.

3. Al O'Connor, Sabbatical Report of Activities (undated but in folder titled "1980"), NIU Steel Band Archive.

4. Al O'Connor, interview by Andrew Martin, November 16, 2012.

5. For more information on the quality of the US Navy Steel Band's instruments, see Martin, *Military Might*, chaps. 1, 3.

6. See Shannon Dudley, *Music from behind the Bridge: Steelband Aesthetics and Politics in Trinidad and Tobago* (New York: Oxford University Press, 2008); Stuempfle, *Steelband Movement*; Ray Funk and Jeannine Remy, *The Invaders Steel Orchestra: The History of a Legendary Steelband* (Port of Spain, Trinidad: Jhullian Graphics, 2015); and Kim Johnson, *The Illustrated Story of Pan* (Port of Spain, Trinidad: University of Trinidad and Tobago Press, 2011).

7. Cliff Alexis, interview by Andrew Martin, November 17, 2012.

8. For information on the term "bad johns," see Kim Johnson, "An Oral and Pictorial History of Pan: Problems and Possibilities," October 16, 2008, lecture given at the National Library in Port of Spain. A synopsis of the lecture is available online at http://www.trinbagopan.com/articles/161008.htm.

9. Cliff Alexis, interview by Jeannine Remy, March 30, 2003.

10. Jeannine Remy, "Hall of Fame: Clifford Alexis," *Percussive Notes* 51, no. 6 (November 2013): 6.

11. Ibid.

12. Funk and Remy, *Invaders Steel Orchestra*.

13. Goddard, *Forty Years in the Steelbands*, 132.

14. For more information on the tour, see George Goddard, *Forty Years in the Steelbands*, 130–40. The National Steelband went on tour to England in 1965 and Canada in 1967.

15. See Frank N. D. Buchman, *Remaking the World* (London, Blandford Press: 1961), Johnston and Sampson, *Religion, the Missing Dimension of Statecraft* (Oxford: Oxford University Press, 1994), and "Timeline," "Initiatives of Change," accessed March 31, 2013, http://www.iofc.org/history/.

16. Staff Writer, *Trinidad Guardian*, August 28, 1964.

17. Ibid.

18. Ibid.

19. Cliff Alexis, interview by Andrew Martin, April 6, 2013.

20. Cliff Alexis, interview by Jeannine Remy, March 30, 2003.

21. Cliff Alexis, interview by Ray Funk, October 29, 2013.

22. Shannon Dudley, Press release, Office of Public Information, Northern Illinois University, undated (1986).

23. Ibid.

24. Advertisement, "Shangoya," Subject Files, Minnesota Culture Archives, Minnesota Historical Society, St. Paul, Minnesota.

25. Al O'Connor, interview by Satanand Sharma, November 6, 2000.

26. Cliff Alexis, interview by Andrew Martin, November 17, 2012.

27. Al O'Connor, interview by Andrew Martin and Ray Funk, April 6, 2013.

28. Al O'Connor, interview by Andrew Martin, November 16, 2012.

29. Ibid.

30. Ibid.

31. Ibid.

NOTES TO CHAPTER 4

1. Emphasis in Original. Al O'Connor memo to Dean Madeja, March 7, 1986, p. 2.

2. Al O'Connor, interview with Andrew Martin, November 16 2012.

3. Al O'Connor memo to Dean Madeja," March 7, 1986, p. 2.
4. Paul Ross, interview by Ray Funk, April 22, 2013.
5. Staff Writer, "Pan Man Makes His Music a Science," *City Sun*, March 19–25, 1986.
6. Jeannine Remy, e-mail to Andrew Martin, June 20, 2013.
7. Al O'Connor, interview by Andrew Martin, November 16, 2012.
8. James Walker, interview by Ray Funk, October 11, 2013.
9. Staff Writer, "Pan Man Makes His Music a Science," *City Sun*, March 19–25, 1986.
10. Ibid.
11. Shannon Dudley, e-mail to Jeannine Remy, June 27, 2013.
12. Cliff Alexis, interview by Andrew Martin, November 17, 2012.
13. Paul Ross, interview by Ray Funk, April 22, 2013.
14. Elizabeth DeLamater, interview by Ray Funk, October 4, 2013.
15. Birch Creek Summer Music Academy program 2012, pp. 50–51.
16. Mike Schwebke, interview by Ray Funk, April 22, 2013.
17. Rich Holly, e-mail to Jeannine Remy, June 27, 2013.
18. James Walker, interview by Ray Funk, October 11, 2013.
19. This included providing stage props (duck calls, whistles, silly hats, etc.) to assist Robert Chappell in winning the xylophone playoff competition, complete with his water galoshes, an umbrella, and any other gimmick to try to win for fun against Gordon Stout. The comedy skit went over so well that Birch Creek incorporated it into one of its evening programs for every percussion session afterwards.
20. Michael Bento, e-mail to Jeannine Remy, March 10, 2013.
21. The factors were mainly racist incidents that Alexis suffered in Sturgeon Bay, Wisconsin, which was the next biggest city.
22. Adam Grise, e-mail to Ray Funk, November 3, 2013.
23. The first recipients of the scholarships in 2013, Avery Attz and Dachelle Morrison, are both from Tobago.

NOTES TO CHAPTER 5

1. Concert transcript, NIU Steelband fall concert, November 18, 2012, transcribed by A. Martin.
2. "Final Rosewood/Steel concert Sunday," *Northern Today* 7, no. 25 (April 2, 1990): 3.
3. Al O'Connor, interview by Andrew Martin and Ray Funk, April 6, 2013.
4. Al O'Connor, interview by Andrew Martin, November 6, 2014.
5. Alexis, too, was a guest soloist of the NIU Steelband in 1984 prior to his official employment by NIU.
6. Al O'Connor, interview by Satanand Sharma, November 6, 2000.
7. Harold Headley, interview with Jeannine Remy, March 6, 2013.
8. Ibid.
9. Al O'Connor, interview with Satanand Sharma, November 6, 2000.
10. Ibid.

NOTES TO CHAPTER 6

1. Jeannine Remy, e-mail to Andrew Martin, April 13, 2013.
2. Ibid.
3. Ibid.
4. Al O'Connor, interview by Andrew Martin and Ray Funk, April 5, 2013.
5. James Campbell, e-mail message to Andrew Martin, June 11, 2016.

6. Al O'Connor, interview by Andrew Martin and Ray Funk, April 6, 2013.

7. "About PAS," Percussive Arts Society, accessed June 18, 2013, http://www.pas.org/About/AboutPAS.aspx.

8. "PASIC 1977 Preview," *Percussive Notes* 16, no. 1 (1977): 16.

9. These include Larry Snider (University of Akron) and Tom Siwe (University of Illinois).

10. Al O'Connor, interview by Andrew Martin and Ray Funk, April 6, 2013.

11. Al O'Connor, interview by Andrew Martin, November 6, 2014.

12. Al O'Connor, interview with Satanand Sharma, November 6, 2000.

13. Ibid.

14. Al O'Connor, interview by Andrew Martin and Ray Funk, April 5, 2013.

15. T. D. Rossing, D. S. Hampton, and J. Boverman, "Acoustics of Caribbean Steel Drums," paper presented at 112th meeting of ASA (1986); D. S. Hampton, C. Alexis, and T. D. Rossing, "Note Coupling in Caribbean Steel Drums," paper presented at 115th meeting of ASA (1987); K. K. Leung, T. D. Rossing, "Sound Spectra of Caribbean Steel Drums," paper presented at Joint Annual Meeting of APS and AAPT, Arlington, VA (1988); T. D. Rossing, D. S. Hampton, and U. J. Hanson, "Acoustics of Steelpans," paper presented at 130th meeting of ASA (1995); and Thomas D. Rossing, D. Scott Hampton, and Uwe J. Hansen, "Music from Oil Drums: The Acoustics of the Steel Pan," *Physics Today* 49, no. 3 (March 1996): 24.

16. Thomas D. Rossing, *The Science of Percussion Instruments* (Singapore: World Scientific, 2000).

17. Letter from Daniel Gallery to Pete Seeger, July 13, 1957, Papers of Admiral Daniel V. Gallery, Special Collections Division, Nimitz Library, United States Naval Academy, Annapolis, Maryland.

18. Cliff Alexis, interview by Andrew Martin, April 5, 2013.

19. Rossing, Hampton, and Hansen, "Music from Oil Drums," 24.

20. Ibid.

21. Staff Writer, "International Pan Conference Next Week," *Trinidad Newsday*, October 14, 2000.

NOTES TO CHAPTER 7

1. Pete Seeger, "The Steel Drum: A New Folk Instrument," *Journal of American Folklore* 71, no. 279 (January–March, 1958): 52–57.

2. Kou-Huang Han, "The Use of the Marian Antiphons in Renaissance Motets" (PhD diss., Evanston, IL: Northwestern University, 1974).

3. Kou-Huang Han, e-mail to Andrew Martin, March 18, 2013.

4. Northern Illinois University, *East Meets West: Chinese and Balinese Music Performed by the Asian Music Ensemble, Northern Illinois University*, Folkways Records FSS37455, 1981.

5. B. J. Sullivan, "America's First Collegiate Steel Band Heads for Another First in Taiwan: Leaves March 11 from Chicago's O'Hare International Airport for Taipei," NIU press release, March 6, 1992.

6. Bernard Holland, "6 Compositions by Ma Shui-Long," *New York Times*, March 23, 1987.

7. Kou-Huang Han, e-mail to Andrew Martin, March 3, 2013.

8. By the time Barnes-Tsai arrived at NIU, the Chinese ensemble was already disbanded. She studied the yangchin, the Chinese hammered dulcimer, with Dr. Han and then continued her study on the American version of the same instrument with a teacher in Chicago from the Old Town School of Folk Music. The repertoire consisted primarily of American and Irish folk music, and Barnes-Tsai chose the hammer dulcimer as the focus of her master's thesis. Sarah Barnes-Tsai, e-mail to Andrew Martin, September 15, 2013.

9. Sarah Barnes-Tsai, e-mail to Andrew Martin, November 11, 2012.

10. Now some twenty-four years later, she is still going strong, and the pan program at Taipei National University of the Arts is thriving. What began as two small steelbands of just six players has evolved into four bands of thirteen players for a total of fifty steelband students at any given time. Each of the steelbands at Taipei National University of the Arts meets once per week for two hours. The ensembles

are reserved for music major students and non-music major students pursuing degrees in art, theatre, and dance. In keeping with the spirit of pan in Trinidad, Barnes-Tsai teaches these ensembles by rote without music notation—though she does on occasion create her own made-up charts with letter names and numbers. At the end of each semester, the Taipei National University of the Arts steelband gives a concert, which is well attended. Since its inception, nearly one thousand students have taken steelband classes at the university, and thousands more have attended the concerts. What's more, these Taiwanese steelband students are enthusiastic about the music of Trinidad, and their performances feature many of the classic and current calypso/soca tunes familiar to the Caribbean, including those by Lord Kitchener, David Rudder, and the like. See also Andrew Martin and Ray Funk, "Taiwan Embraces Pan and Calypso," *Trinidad Guardian*, April 5, 2013.

11. It was because of Tzong-Ching Ju's affiliation with the National Concert Hall that the NIU performance at the space was arranged. The National Concert Hall performance in 1992 is, perhaps, the most important performance of the Taiwan tours (both 1992 and 1998). Sarah Barnes-Tsai, e-mail to Andrew Martin, September 15, 2013.

12. Tzong-Ching Ju, fax to O'Connor, May 7, 1991, no. 309.
13. Al O'Connor, interview by Andrew Martin, November 16, 2012.
14. 14   .Tzong-Ching Ju, fax to O'Connor, May 7, 1992, no. 309.
15. Sarah Barnes-Tsai, e-mail to Andrew Martin, November 10, 2012.
16. Staff Writer, "It's Encores for the Steel Drums in Taiwan," *Northern News*, Summer 1998.
17. Al O'Connor, interview by Andrew Martin, November 16, 2012.
18. Al O'Connor, interview by Satanand Sharma, November 6, 2000.
19. Memorandum from O'Connor to Jerrold Zar, "Financial Support for Travel in FY92," July 15, 1991, NIU Steelband Archive.
20. Sarah Barnes-Tsai, e-mail to Andrew Martin, November 11, 2012.
21. The addition of these pans would double the size of the TNUA steelband from six sets of pans to twelve—its current size. See Barnes-Tsai, e-mail to Andrew Martin, September 15, 2013.
22. Sarah Barnes-Tsai, e-mail to Andrew Martin, Nov 10, 2012.
23. Cliff Alexis, interview by Andrew Martin, April 7, 2013.
24. "Pan Takes Taiwan by Storm: But from the U.S., not Trinidad," *Sunday Punch*, August 2, 1992.
25. Ju Percussion Foundation, fax to G. Allan O'Connor, December 26, 1991.
26. John Bush, "Jeri Southern," "Allmusic.com," accessed May 20, 2013, http://www.allmusic.com/artist/jeri-southern-mn0000324819.
27. Robert Chappell, interview by Satanand Sharma, December 5, 2000.
28. PASIC 1994 official program.
29. Terry Joseph, "Unknown Band Trounces Trinis," *Trinidad Express*, October 14, 2000.
30. Staff Writer, "It's Encores for the Steel Drums in Taiwan," *Northern News*, Summer 1998.
31. Ibid.
32. Ibid.
33. Ibid.
34. Lester Trilla, letter to NIU April 2, 1998, and letter from O'Connor to NIU Foundation January 19, 1998, NIU Steelband Archive.
35. Paulina Milana, "Encore! Invited for Repeat Performance, NIU's Steel Band Takes It to Taiwan," *Northern Today*, March 2, 1998.
36. Al O'Connor, "1998 Taiwan Tour Itinerary," NIU Steelband Archive.
37. Northern Illinois University Steelband, "Liner Notes," *Return to Taiwan: The NIU Steelband*, NITT98, 1998.
38. Veronica Gonzalez, "NIU Steel Drummers Had It 'Made in Taiwan,'" *Weekender* (DeKalb), April 17, 1998.

39. A sample of articles critical of the NIU Steelband's success in Taiwan can be found in the University of the West Indies—St. Augustine digital *Steelpan Newspaper Clippings* database. See the database itself at http://uwispace.sta.uwi.edu/dspace/handle/2139/17577 for more information.

40. Jessica Majkowski, "Steel Band to Keep the Beat at World Cup," *Northern Star* 102, no. 138 (April 24, 2002): 1.

41. Rob Carroll, "Steel Band to Represent American in South Korea," *Saturday Chronicle* (DeKalb), April 27, 2002, p. 1.

42. Adam Grise, interview by Ray Funk, November 1, 2013.

NOTES TO CHAPTER 8

1. Liam Teague, letter to O'Connor, May 20, 1992.
2. Diane Strand, Memo, "NIU Steelband Founder Al O'Connor Named Associate Dean," Office of Public Relations, August 18, 1989, Northern Illinois University, p. 1.
3. Richard Forteau, letter to Al O'Connor, July 20, 1989.
4. World Steel Band Music Festival commemorative program, October 2000.
5. John McDonald Jr., e-mail to Andrew Martin, January 30, 2013. See also "Captain McDonald," "Citizen's Hose Company," accessed April 8, 2013, http://www.citizenshosecompany.com/band_captain_mcdonald.cfm.
6. Jeannine Remy, "An Interview with G. Allan O'Connor," *Percussive Notes* 35, no. 2 (February 1994): 29–23, 34–38.
7. Al O'Connor, interview by Andrew Martin, November 17, 2012.
8. Ibid.
9. Remy, "An Interview with G. Allan O'Connor," 35.
10. "Shot Heard Round the World," "Soccer365.com," accessed April 8, 2013, http://www.soccer365.com/today_in_history/129.
11. David Abdulah, "More Respect for School Pan Festival," *Trinidad Express*, November 27, 1989, final edition.
12. "Let's Keep the Tradition Alive," *Trinidad Express*, November 27, 1989, final edition.
13. Ibid.
14. Al O'Connor, interview by Andrew Martin, November 16, 2012.
15. Ibid.
16. Liam Teague, e-mail with Andrew Martin, Ray Funk, and Jeannine Remy, November 10, 2013.
17. Ibid.
18. Liam Teague, interview by Andrew Martin, November 17, 2012.
19. Al O'Connor, interview by Andrew Martin, November 16, 2012.
20. Liam Teague, interview by Andrew Martin, November 17, 2012.
21. Liam Teague, letter to Al O'Connor, May 20, 1992.
22. Ibid.
23. Staff Writer, "Liam Teague Benefit Concert," *Trinidad Guardian*, October 24, 1992.
24. Al O'Connor, interview by Andrew Martin, November 16, 2012.
25. Ibid.
26. Al O'Connor, memo to Madeja, March 7, 1986, p. 2, NIU Steelband Archive.
27. Les Trilla, interview by Andrew Martin, November 20, 2012.
28. "2010 NIU Foundation Award for Lifetime Giving Lester Trilla," NIUFoundation.org, accessed January 12, 2013, http://www.niufoundation.org/lester-trilla.
29. Cliff Alexis, interview by Andrew Martin, November 17, 2012.
30. Ibid.

31. "2010 NIU Foundation Award for Lifetime Giving Lester Trilla," NIUFoundation.org.
32. Les Trilla, interview by Andrew Martin, November 18, 2012.
33. Al O'Connor, interview by Andrew Martin, November 16, 2012.
34. "2010 NIU Foundation Award for Lifetime Giving Lester Trilla," NIUFoundation.org.
35. Ibid.
36. Kenneth Joseph, telephone interview by Ray Funk, October 7, 2013.
37. Staff Writer, "Teague Gets Scholarship from Enron," *Trinidad Express*, August 29, 1997.

NOTES TO CHAPTER 9

1. Sean Nero, "NIU Making Pans in Trinidad," *Trinidad Newsday*, October 11, 2000.
2. See World Steelband Music Festival official program, 2000, p. 2; and Johnson, *Illustrated Story of Pan*, chap. 2.
3. World Steelband Music Festival official program, 2000.
4. Terry Joseph, "Festival, Not Panorama," *Trinidad Express*, October 11, 2000.
5. Cliff Alexis, interview with Andrew Martin, November 17, 2012.
6. Nero, "NIU Making Pans in Trinidad."
7. Ibid.
8. Al O'Connor, interview with Andrew Martin, April 6, 2013.
9. Nero, "NIU Making Pans in Trinidad.".
10. Letter from WSMF, September 15, 2000, to O'Connor and Alexis Held, NIU Steelband Archive.
11. Sean Nero, "Increase of Prizes Not Likely Says Arnold," *Trinidad Express*, October 3, 2000.
12. Al O'Connor, letter to Amerijet, August 16, 2000, NIU Steelband Archive.
13. Nero, "NIU Making Pans in Trinidad."
14. "Pannists Prefer to Practice in Yards," *Trinidad Guardian*, October 19, 20005.
15. See Andrew Martin and Ray Funk, "French Steelband Undeterred by Attacks," *Trinidad Guardian*, November 26, 2015, http://www.guardian.co.tt/lifestyle/2015-11-26/french-steelband-undeterred-attacks.
16. Ibid.
17. While judging Pan Is Beautiful IX in 1998, O'Connor observed a major controversy over using a sampled keyboard to produce the sound of cannon shots when the Invaders Steelband played their rendition of "Wellington's Victory."
18. World Steelband Music Festival 2000 Test Piece Queries–Dawn of the Millennium, NIU Steelband Archive.
19. Terry Joseph, "Unknown Band Trounces Trinis," *Trinidad Express*, October 14, 2000.
20. Jeannine Remy, e-mail to Andrew Martin, September 10, 2013.
21. Peter Blood, "Steelband Festival Signals," *Trinidad Guardian*, October 21, 2000.
22. Keith Smith, "A Night of Dreams," *Trinidad Express*, October 23, 2000.
23. Jeannine Remy, e-mail to Andrew Martin, September 11, 2013.
24. Press release, Northern Illinois University Office of Public Affairs, "NIU Steel Band Takes Second Place in International Contest," October 24, 2000.
25. Ibid.
26. Nearly a month passed following the conclusion of the WSMF without any prize monies being distributed. A total of $3,000,000 TTD ($500,000 USD) was outstanding to steelbands, suppliers of goods, transportation companies, and other service contractors patronized by the festival. Delays in such allocations are rather commonplace in Trinidad; however, for the foreign bands participating in the WSMF the situation was frustrating. *Trinidad Express* columnist Terry Joseph lambasted the situation stating "Bands, particularly those that incurred massive debts to make the trip from far-flung countries, have now passed the stage of polite queries and are now becoming angry over not being paid their prize money and appearance fees." Patrick

Arnold of Pan Trinbago was quoted as saying "The situation has really become quite embarrassing, because the bands left without their money on the basis of trust." Terry Joseph, "No Sign of Prize Money," *Trinidad Express*, November 9, 2000.

27. Al O'Connor, e-mail to Jeannine Remy, June 23, 2013.
28. Peter Blood, "Steelband Festival Signals," *Trinidad Guardian*, October 21, 2000.
29. Terry Joseph, "Sharpe and Skiffle Winning Since 1984," *Trinidad Express*, October 23, 2000.
30. Press release, Northern Illinois University Office of Public Affairs, "NIU Steel Band Takes Second Place in International Contest," October 24, 2000.
31. Terry Joseph, "Skiffle Bunch Brings It Home," *Trinidad Express*, October 23, 2000.
32. Press release, Northern Illinois University Office of Public Affairs, "NIU Steel Band Takes Second Place in International Contest," October 24, 2000.
33. Ibid.

NOTES TO CHAPTER 10

1. "Pan Goes to University," *Trinidad Guardian*, November 25, 1989.
2. "US Music Professor Hails the Steeldrum," *Trinidad Guardian*, February 25, 1986.
3. Ibid.
4. Janine Louise Tiffe, "Trinidadian Steel Drum (Pan) Bands in Three Great Lakes States: A Study of Musical Migration" (master's thesis, Kent State University, 2006), 59.
5. It should be noted, however, that neither Paulette Frazier nor Twyla Cole completed a degree in music at NIU.
6. Harold Headley, interview by Jeannine Remy, March 6, 2013.
7. Ibid.
8. Ibid.
9. Herold Headley, "Proposal for Individualized Major for Harold Headley," NIU Steelband Archive, 1989.
10. Seion Gomez, interview by Jeannine Remy, April 21, 2013.
11. Harold Headley, interview by Jeannine Remy, March 6, 2013.
12. "Steelband Footnote," *Trinidad Guardian*, November 26, 1989.
13. "Pan Goes to University," *Trinidad Guardian*, November 25, 1989.
14. Dr. Osborne led the committee to write the curriculum, which included Rawle Gibbons, Mervyn Williams, Merle Albino De Coteau, June Joseph, Sandra Gift, Richard Forteau, and Jocelyn Loncke.
15. Jeannine Remy, "Pan in the 21st Century: Steelpan Repertoire in the Professional Market," *Percussive Notes* 49, no. 2 (March 2011): 4–7.
16. Rich Holly, e-mail to Jeannine Remy, July 3, 2013.
17. Satanand Sharma, e-mail to Jeannine Remy, June 28, 2013.
18. "NIU Steel Band Welcomes Trinidad Ambassador for Nov. 20 Concert, Exploration of Partnerships," *NIU Today*, November 14, 2011.

NOTES TO CHAPTER 11

1. "NIU Percussion News and Events," NIU.edu, accessed July 1, 2013, http://www.niu.edu/music/areas_of_study/percussion/archive.shtml.
2. Al O'Connor, interview by Andrew Martin, November 18, 2012.
3. Rich Holly, interview by Andrew Martin, November 18, 2012.
4. Elizabeth DeLamater, telephone interview by Ray Funk, October 4, 2013.

5. "Composer Jan Bach and the Steelpan," "When Steel Talks," accessed October 25, 2013, http://www.panonthenet.com/spotlight/2009/ian_bach-5-6-09.htm.

6. Ibid.

7. Jan Bach, e-mail to Ray Funk, October 18, 2013.

8. Ultimately, the commission was supported by the financial assistance of the Woodstock Chimes Foundation, Garry and Diane Kvistad, presidents. See "Program Notes," JanBach.com, accessed October 17, 2013, http://www.janbach.com/page87.html. Al O'Connor was also actively involved in arranging the commission.

9. "Composer Jan Bach and Steel Pan," When Steel Talks.

10. Sarah Bryan Miller, "Personal Notes: A Conversation with Composer Jan Bach," *Chicago Reader*, April 5, 1996.

11. John von Rhein, "Steelpan Concerto Just Exhilarating," *Chicago Tribune*, November 15, 1995.

12. *Paul Freeman introduces Exotic Concertos*, Albany 521 (2002).

13. Jan Bach, *Concerto for Steelpan and Orchestra, Paul Freeman Introduces Exotic Concertos*, vol. 9, Albany Records, 2002.

14. Liam Teague e-mail to Andrew Martin, March 20, 2009.

15. Staff Writer, "Liam Teague—The Paganini of Pan," *Trinidad Newsday*, July 3, 1997.

16. Liam Teague, e-mail to Ray Funk, October 29, 2013.

17. Staff Writer, "Teague," *Trinidad Express*, June 6, 2004.

18. Libby Larson, *Concertino for Tenor Steel Drum and Chamber Orchestra*, LibbyLarson.com, accessed March 17, 2016, http://libbylarsen.com/index.php?contentID=242&profileID=1244&startRange.

19. Deborah Fischer Teason, "Composer," dfteason.com, accessed March 17, 2016, http://www.dfteason.com/composer.html.

20. "Kevin Bobo," "Indiana University: Jacobs School of Music," accessed March 17, 2016, http://info.music.indiana.edu/faculty/current/bobo-kevin.shtml.

21. Ibid.

22. Terry Joseph, "Teague: Music Literacy No Must for Pannists," *Trinidad Express*, June 16, 2000.

23. Liam Teague, e-mail to Andrew Martin, July 2, 2013.

24. Rich Holly, e-mail to Andrew Martin, July 3, 2013.

25. Terry Joseph, "Teague Plays Another One for Pan," *Trinidad Express*, April 23, 2001.

26. Terry Joseph, "Teague Takes Over," *Trinidad Express*, August 8, 2003.

27. Ibid.

28. Press release, "NIU Steel Band to Celebrate Three Decades with Special Concert," *NIU News*, March 31, 2003.

29. Howard Reich, "Steelpan Alley: To Become A Virtuoso on the Steel Drum, Liam Teague Had to Leave His Native Trinidad to Study in—Where Else?—DeKalb," *Chicago Tribune*, June 27, 1999.

30. Stephanie Szuda, "A Panoramic View of Music," *Northern Star*, November 17, 2005, http://northernstar.info/dekalb_scene/article_f8bbcf8c-9e1c-5db0-8e59-60d01121c5cd.html.

31. "Jazz Studies," NIU.edu, accessed November 4, 2013, http://www.niu.edu/music/areas_of_study/jazzstudies.shtml.

32. Neil Tesser, "Neville York," Chicagoreader.com, accessed November 4, 2013, http://www.chicagoreader.com/chicago/neville-york/Content?oid=907496.

33. Mike Schwebke, telephone interview by Ray Funk, November 1, 2013.

34. Liam Teague, e-mail to Ray Funk, November 2, 2013.

35. Chonze Maddox, "Icon Ron Carter to Conduct His Last NIU Jazz Ensemble Concert," "NIU Today," accessed March 17, 2016, http://www.niutoday.info/2014/04/07/icon-ron-carter-to-conduct-his-last-niu-jazz-ensemble-concert/.

36. Victor Provost, telephone interview with Ray Funk, November 4, 2013.

37. In 2008 Teague performed for the Panorama finals with the Buccooneers Steel Orchestra led by NIU graduate Seion Gomez.

38. "Arranger Liam Teague—on Panorama 2012 & more," "When Steel Talks," accessed April 1, 2016, http://www.panonthenet.com/tnt/2012/interviews/liam-teague-invue-panorama-1-9-2012.htm.

39. "Liam Teague on Panorama 2016: Up-Close!," When Steel Talks, accessed April 1, 2016, http://www.panonthenet.com/tnt/2016/upclose/liam-teague-2016.htm#sthash.48bmXD3p.dpuf.

40. "Arranger Liam Teague—on Panorama 2012 & more," When Steel Talks.

41. "Liam Teague on Panorama 2016: Up-Close!," When Steel Talks.

NOTES TO CHAPTER 12

1. Charissa Granger, interview by Ray Funk, October 31, 2013.

2. Press release, "NIU Steel Band to Celebrate Three Decades with Special Concert," *NIU News*, March 31, 2003.

3. "Steel Panist Liam Teague Speaks on NIU's Latest Project," When Steel Talks, accessed October 31, 2013, http://www.panonthenet.com/spotlight/2007/05-08-07_liam.htm.

4. The NIU steelband program had tried to add a third steelband a few years earlier, but the effort fell flat and was not able to be sustained. Yuko Asada, telephone interview by Ray Funk, October 31, 2013.

5. "Community School of the Arts," "Northern Illinois University Office of External Programs," accessed May 19, 2016, http://www.niu.edu/extprograms/arts/index.shtml.

6. Ibid.

7. Jeffrey Ross Thomas, *Forty Years of Steel: An Annotated Discography of Steel Band and Pan Recordings, 1951–1991* (Westport, CT: Greenwood Press, 1992); Jeffrey Ross Thomas, "A History of Pan and the Evolution of the Steel Band in Trinidad and Tobago," (master's thesis, Wesleyan University, 1986).

8. Dan Nichols, e-mail to Ray Funk, March 29, 2013. For more information on the NIU YouTube channel, see http://www.youtube.com/niusomofficial.

9. Rich Holly, e-mail to Andrew Martin, April 18, 2013.

10. Rich Holly, "NIU Steel Band Concert a Huge Success," The Arts @ NIU, accessed April 20, 2013, http://niucvpa.blogspot.com/2010/04/niu-steel-band-concert-huge-success.html.

11. Sean Nero, "Panguard Honored," *Trinidad Guardian*, November 24, 2006.

12. "Outstanding Service Award," Northern Illinois University Operating Staff Council, accessed April 20, 2013, http://www.niu.edu/osc/serviceaward/2009/CAlexis.shtml.

13. "NIU Steel Drum Musician Cliff Alexis Collects Two Emmy Nominations for 'Hammer on Steel,'" *NIU Today*, May 15, 2012, http://www.niutoday.info/2012/05/15/niu-steel-drum-musician-cliff-alexis-collects-two-emmy-nominations-for-hammer-on-steel/.

14. "NIU Steelpan Maker, Artist Cliff Alexis Selected for 2013 Percussive Arts Society Hall of Fame," NIU Today, June 24, 2013, http://www.niutoday.info/2013/06/24/niu-steelpan-maker-artist-cliff-alexis-selected-for-2013-percussive-arts-society-hall-of-fame/.

15. Jeannine Remy, "Hall of Fame: Clifford Alexis," *Percussive Notes* 51, no. 6 (November 2013): 6.

16. "Liam Teague Wins Homeland Honors," *NIU Today*, August 31, 2012, http://www.niutoday.info/2012/08/31/musics-liam-teague-wins-homeland-honors/.

17. Ibid.

18. "PANFest 2016," *vafest.org*, accessed May 24, 2016, http://vafest.com/panfest-2016.

19. Liam Teague, e-mail to Andrew Martin, February 12, 2016.

20. Yuko Asada, e-mail to Andrew Martin, February 15, 2016.

INDEX

Aarons, Davis, 102
Abdullah, David, 81
Abel, Jeff, 16
Acoustical Society of America, 9, 55, 62–65
All University Steelband, 119
Antigua, 14, 121, 138n14
Asada, Yuko, xi, 41, 44, 120, 127, 147n4, 147n20
Arnold, Patrick, 26–28, 91, 94, 144n11, 145n26
Aruba, 14, 19, 29

Babb, Randolph "Ronnie," 24
Bach, Jan, xi, 104–110, 112, 129, 135, 146n5–10, 146n13
Barnes-Tsai, Sarah, xi, 67–70, 98, 141n8–10, 142n11, 142n15, 142n20–22
Bauer, Paul, 96, 111
Belafonte, Harry, 13
Bento, Michael, xi, 17, 43, 138n19, 140n20
Black Earth Percussion Group, 31
Blood, Peter, 94
Borde, Hugh, 27
Bobo, Kevin, 62, 109
Bruno, Wayne, 102
Brute Force Steelband, 14, 131, 138n14
Bush, Jeff, 98
BWIA Sunjets, 26–28
Byers, Gregory, 109

CAFÉ (Cultural Academy for Excellence), 45
Calypso, 3–4, 7, 36, 42–43, 56–57, 60, 71–75, 81, 90, 92, 107, 109, 112, 125–126, 129, 131, 137n9
Calypsociation, 92
Campbell, James, 61, 98
Carnival, 3–4, 6, 12, 24, 26, 80, 114, 121
Carson, Joe, 84
Carter, Ron, 112–113
Chappell, Robert, xi, 41, 43, 61–62, 68, 70–72, 74–75, 92–93, 112, 126, 128–129, 135, 140n19, 142n27
Charles, Etienne, 53
Check, Frank, 121
Chicago Sinfonietta de Camera, 8, 106
Cole, Twyla, 34, 98
Cook, Gary, 34
Cordice, Khan, 102, 121
Dale, Doug, 34
de Labastide, Andrew, 7
de Las, Khion, 102
DeLamater, Elizabeth, xi, 38–39, 41, 104, 121, 140n14, 145n4
Desperadoes Steel Orchestra, 51
Dudley, Shannon, xi, 19, 37–38, 139n6, 139n22, 140n11
Dutton, James, 40, 42

Electronic Music, 13–15, 138n5
Electric Stereopticon, 14, 138n13

Fernandez, Gerard, 24
Flocker-Aming, Liz, 102
Forteau, Richard, 90
Francis, Josanne, 121
Frazier, Paulette, 34, 98, 121
Freeberg, Ed, 87

Granger, Charissa, 117
Gallery, Daniel (Admiral), 62, 141n17
Goddard, George, 25, 137n5, 139n13–14
Gomez, Seion, 100, 102
Gonzalez, Nadine, 102
Gormandy, Mia, 122
Greenidge, Robert, 52, 107, 112–113
Grise, Adam, 76

Hammer on Steel, 123
Han, Kou-Huang, 65, 141n2–3, 141n7
Hanning, Chris, 62
Headley, Harold, xi, 10, 19, 51–52, 91, 99–100, 102, 121, 140n7, 145n6
Hell's Gate, 14
Hill 60 Steel Band, 23
Hillside Symphony, 114
Hit Paraders, 23–24
Holly, Rich, xi, 17, 41, 68, 70, 74, 102, 104, 112, 140n17, 145n16, 145n31, 146n24, 147n9
Holman, Ray, 52, 61, 125, 132, 134

Invaders Steel Orchestra, 6, 23–25, 28, 94, 139n6, 139, n12, 144n17
Jazz, 10, 14, 19, 40–41, 43, 49, 52–53, 56, 72, 99–100, 109–110, 112–114, 146n31
Joseph, Kenneth, 87, 102
Joylanders, 24
Ju, Czong-Ching, 67
Ju Percussion Group, 68–74, 142n25

Kafer, Howard, 106
King, Kareem "TJ," 102

Larson, Libby, 108
Lee, Jenny, 92
Leith, Akua, 102
Lewis, Sean, 99
Liberace, 27
Little Carib Theatre, The, 6, 137n6
Loquan, Mark. 45

Lowe, Denise, 102
Ma, Shui-Long, 66
Madeja, Stanley, 34
Magnus, Gay, 102
Mannette, Barry, 102, 121
Mannette, Ellie, 7, 24–25, 28, 61–62
Marshall, Bertie, 56
Martirano, Salvatore, 12
McBurnie, Beryl, 6, 137n6
McDonald, John (Captain), 80, 143n5
McIntosh, Louise, 99
Merry Makers Steel Orchestra, 6, 129
Mint Condition, 29, 244
Mohammed, Lennox "Bobby," 25
Moral Re-Armament, 26
Moses, Leonard, vii, xi, 50–52, 60, 98, 100, 121, 126
Murphy, Richard, 90, 96
Music Literacy Trust, 109

Narell, Andy, vii, 29, 49–50, 52, 107, 113, 126, 133
National Schools Steelband Competition, 80, 90
National Steelband Music Festival, 83
National Steelband of Trinidad and Tobago, 25
NIU Community School of the Arts Steelband, 119–121

O'Connor, Ethan, 75
Osborne, Anne, 90, 102, 145n14
Oshkosh (Wisconsin), 51, 99
Our Boys, 50

PANFest, vii, 120, 123, 147n18
Pan is Beautiful, 80, 89–90, 94, 144n17
Pan Pipers Pan School, 99
Pan Trinbago, xi, 25, 63, 80, 89–94, 101, 123, 139n8, 145n26
Panorama, 3–4, 22, 36, 44, 60, 74, 80, 100, 109, 114–115, 121, 123, 137n7, 144n4, 147n37–41
PASIC (Percussive Arts Society International Convention), 9, 50, 55, 58–62, 65, 123, 141n8, 142n28
Patcheye, 24
Pouchet, Edwin, 25, 114
Prospect, Anthony, 97
Provost, Victor, 53, 113

Rubin, Jeff, 14, 15
Regrello, Junia, 90
Reich, Howard, 8
Remy, Jeannine, 19, 36, 56, 94, 98, 102

Richards, George, 19, 21–22, 30
Riley, Emmanuel "Cobo Jack," 24
Robinson, Talib, 121
Rosewood-n-Steel, 17, 48
Ross, Jeffrey Thomas, 121
Ross, Paul, xi, 34, 38–39, 94, 121, 140n4
Rossing, Thomas, 62–64, 141n15–16, 141n19
Rudder, David, 49, 53, 60, 128, 131, 134, 142n10

Scales, Jonathan, 48, 53
Schwebke, Mike, xi, 40, 113, 140n16, 146n33
Seeger, Pete, 8, 62, 65, 138n14, 141n17, 141n1
Sharma, Satanand, xi, 91, 95, 102, 121, 138n4, 139n25, 140n6, 140n9, 141n12, 142n18, 142n27, 145n17
Sharpe, Len "Boogsie," 44, 50–52, 60–61, 72, 74, 92, 95, 113, 126–128, 133–134, 145
Sheppard, Darren, 82
Simon, Winston "Spree," 7
Siwe, Tom, 12, 40, 52
Skiffle Bunch, 95, 114
Smith, Rudy "Two Left," 52, 113
Snider, Larry, 12, 61
Steelpan European, 92
Starlift, 114
Stereophonics, 24
Steil, Cynthia and Carol, 110
Stitely, Jeff, 41
St. Paul (Minnesota), 9, 23, 27–30, 34–35, 98, 139n24
St. Paul Central High School, vii, 27–28
Subero, Sophia, 102

Taipei National University of the Arts, 66–67, 141n10
Tamboo Bamboo, 6
Tanner, Chris, 53

Tarradath, Selwyn, 80
Teague, Russell, 80
Thomas, Leon Foster, 53, 113
Transcriptions and Arrangements, 11, 15, 24, 27, 36–38, 42–44, 50, 57, 60–61, 67–69, 73–74, 80, 86, 90, 92–93, 106, 109, 112–114, 119, 121
Trilla, Lester, vii, ix, xi, 74, 85–87, 102, 117–118, 142n34, 143n27–28, 144n31–32, 144n34
Trinidad All-Steel Percussion Orchestra (TASPO), 6, 89
Trinidad and Tobago Folk Arts Institute, 110
Trinidad and Tobago National Steel Orchestra, vii, 25–26, 51, 122
Tripoli Steel Band, 24, 27, 51, 99

Udow, Michael, 12
US Navy Steel Band, 9, 14, 22–23, 28, 49, 52, 62, 85
US Virgin Islands, ix, 13

Wahland, Ben, 41, 109
Walker, James, 37, 41
Webcast, 122
Wells, Rudolph, 93
When Steel Talks, 122, 146n5, 146n9, 147n38–41, 147n3
White, Andre, 53
Williams, Anthiny, 7
Wood-n-Steel, 61, 71–74, 92–96, 126n4, 135
Wordel, Lana, 37
World Cup Soccer, 9, 65, 75–77, 81, 103, 143n40

Yorke, Neville, 113, 121

Zephryrine, Errol, 24